CAREER COMEDOWN

CAREER COMEDOWN

What to Do
When Work Isn't
Working for You

Stefanie Sword-Williams

4th ESTATE • *London*

4th Estate
An imprint of HarperCollins*Publishers*
1 London Bridge Street
London SE1 9GF

www.4thestate.co.uk

HarperCollins*Publishers*
Macken House
39/40 Mayor Street Upper
Dublin 1
D01 C9W8
Ireland

First published in Great Britain in 2026 by 4th Estate

1

Copyright © Stefanie Sword-Williams, 2026

Stefanie Sword-Williams asserts the moral right to be identified as the author of this work in accordance with the Copyright, Designs and Patents Act 1988

A catalogue record for this book is available from the British Library

ISBN 978-0-00-870634-0 (hardback)
ISBN 978-0-00-870635-7 (trade paperback)

All rights reserved. No part of this publication may be reproduced, stored in a retrieval system, or transmitted, in any form or by any means, electronic, mechanical, photocopying, recording or otherwise, without the prior permission of the publishers.

Without limiting the author's and publisher's exclusive rights, any unauthorised use of this publication to train generative artificial intelligence (AI) technologies is expressly prohibited. HarperCollins also exercise their rights under Article 4(3) of the Digital Single Market Directive 2019/790 and expressly reserve this publication from the text and data mining exception.

Typeset in 11.45/15.25pt Adobe Garamond Pro by Six Red Marbles UK, Thetford, Norfolk

Printed and bound in Great Britain by CPI Group (UK) Ltd, Croydon

This book contains FSC™ certified paper and other controlled sources to ensure responsible forest management.

For more information visit: www.harpercollins.co.uk/green

For those brave enough to question their relationship with work, and courageous enough to change it. This book is for you.

CAREER COMEDOWN

CONTENTS

Introduction	1
1. What is Career Comedown?	7
2. The Audit	19
3. Stick	33
4. Twist	105
5. Tap Out	161
6. Post-Audit	233
7. What's Next	239
8. Conclusion	245
Endnotes	249
Acknowledgements	255

INTRODUCTION

One morning in July 2023, I shared a post on Instagram that led to hundreds of notifications within an hour of it going live. It wasn't a planned post – in fact, it was shared in the middle of summer when social media engagement can be dry – but it ended up being the most engaged piece of content I'd put out all year. I was inundated with comments and DMs from people telling me that this was it, this was the feeling they hadn't been able to put into words themselves. I had touched a nerve.

The post was captioned: 'Are you having a career comedown?' and it read:

> *You've spent your 20's climbing the so-called career ladder, you've had a couple of pay rises, a promotion, and on paper everything seems glowing. But, you're still not feeling fulfilled. You know that the future looks much of the same, and it ain't giving you that get-up out-of-bed energy. The harsh realities of your chosen industry are becoming pretty hard to ignore, but you've never really entertained doing anything else. So even if you did want to change directions, you genuinely have no idea where to turn. All you know is you want to get out of the rat race, because you know even when you get to the highest point you'll still question . . . 'Is this it?'*

CAREER COMEDOWN

A career comedown is not a quarter-life crisis (the wobble you have at the start of your career as you transition into adulthood). It is the experience of investing time and energy into your career, seeing positive results and yet still feeling like it's not enough. It's the feeling of motivation slipping away whilst you continue to clock in the hours. When I shared my definition that day, I honestly had no idea that it would be met with a sea of people crying out for help: 'This is a perfect definition', 'Omg yes, this is hitting me hard right now' and 'I'm nodding so hard my head might come loose'. I couldn't believe how vulnerable, open and honest people were being; it's one thing for people to acknowledge the feeling of career comedown to themselves, but another entirely to publicly share how deeply it's been impacting them. Some people felt worried about leaving jobs, others thought about quitting altogether, and many blamed external factors (from the pandemic to the economic crisis) for leading them towards an existential crisis. Whatever the specifics, it was clear that this was a big problem.

At that time, I didn't try to offer solutions, which is extremely out of character for me. Over the last eight years, I've built an international business and movement named F*ck Being Humble, with the goal of helping as many people get what they deserve in their careers as possible. As a public speaker, I've delivered talks that have reached people in more than fifty countries and have been trusted by some of the world's largest companies – Apple, Netflix, Nike, Adidas, Google and Diageo – to empower their employees in their careers. As a leader in my field, I've been named as one of the Top 50 Workplace Leaders in the UK, was recognised in the *Forbes* 30 Under 30 list for Europe, and won LinkedIn's Future Is Female Award for my dedication to uplifting and mentoring people on their professional journeys. Every

INTRODUCTION

day I share advice, tools and strategies to help tackle career problems, but on this occasion, before I sprang into action, I wanted to uncover the true extent of how career comedown was impacting people.

To begin with, I arranged interviews with a range of people who had commented on my initial post, asking them to describe their experiences with the working world and to share why the phrase 'career comedown' resonated with them so much. The unanimous response was that work was no longer working for them in its current form, and they needed to find a way to create a career that felt more suited to what they care about and that met their needs.

Something clicked, and I could not let this idea go. From that point on, I brought up that I was writing a book proposal at every networking event, social gathering or workplace discussion I attended in order to gauge the response. I was met with nods every single time. Either the person I was speaking to was suffering with career comedown or they knew someone else who was. Mid-presentation at one of my F*ck Being Humble community events, I decided to ask my audience: 'How many of you are happy with your career right now?' Only one person out of fifty-five people said yes. One out of fifty-five! I'd say I was shocked but, by this point, it was what I'd come to expect.

It's not just the on-the-ground insights that confirmed my thinking. I've spent months reading studies, articles, reports, surveys and online content explaining how exactly we got here. From an ever-changing working world to a global mental health crisis, looming recessions and unpredictable job security, we are all, unsurprisingly, constantly being forced to reassess what we want and need from our careers. In the UK, The Living Wage Foundation produced a report explaining that 'insecure work' – the fear or concern that an individual has about losing their job – is a key feature of the UK economy, with over six million workers experiencing some form of work insecurity.[1] In the US, the labour market saw tremendous spikes in job shifts in 2019–22, reporting that there were 8.6 million career changes, a 50 per cent increase from the last three-year period, according to McKinsey.[2]

The traditional career ladder no longer makes sense and people are, for the first time in living memory, looking to move sideways, diagonally, or what we would traditionally consider down in pursuit of a better working life. This led executive director at Newton Venture Program, Eleanor Kaye, to coin the phrase 'career lattice'. In article for *Stylist* magazine titled 'Why you should make a career lattice rather than climbing the ladder' Eleanor explains that up is no longer always best: 'Our cultural preoccupation with job status and financial metrics keeps too many people in jobs they don't enjoy, trapped by the golden handcuffs of their salary or by the fear of what other people will think. Why shouldn't a banker retrain as a childminder? Or an architect decide to join a startup? Do away with the idea of what society thinks is acceptable. The only thing that matters is what you'll find fulfilling now and in the future.'[3]

So, how do we get out of a career comedown? This book draws on hundreds of hours of conversations, as well as mountains of psychological and organisational research, to offer a method to overcome overwhelm and simplify the decision-making process when reconsidering your career. Using a method I call Stick, Twist or Tap Out, I'll guide you through what to do when work isn't working for you in clear, actionable steps and will help you identify what you want for the next stage in your life, whilst giving you the tools to go out

INTRODUCTION

and get it. If you find yourself dreading the thought of going to work, feel disconnected, or are working towards something that doesn't feel like the dream it once did, this book will guide you to recentre your needs and build a career that really works for you.

CHAPTER 1
WHAT IS CAREER COMEDOWN?

It's a privilege to be able to seize the day and follow our dreams, but what happens when the dreams we've spent so long pursuing don't actually live up to our expectations? My definition of 'Career Comedown' is this:

Career Comedown (noun) – when you invest a significant amount of time and energy in your career, only to realise it doesn't align with your values, lifestyle or present ambitions. A consistent questioning of, 'Is this all there is?'

I'm not going to try to convince you that discontentment at work is entirely new – I'm sure the feeling is as old as work itself – but each generation seems to be feeling it more acutely. Baby boomers had to deal with technology disrupting the very jobs they thought would last forever. Millennials, on the other hand, found themselves caught between the 'stick it out for the pension' mindset of their boomer parents whilst watching Gen-Z swoop in with clear, non-negotiable boundaries that, frankly, us millennials wish we had the courage to set. And Gen-Z had to enter a post-pandemic world that's still figuring itself out. The economy is a mess, job stability is more of a dream than a reality, and no one really knows how to obtain that elusive 'work-life balance' we all keep referencing. Each generation is bombarded with messages like, 'You can do anything if you put your mind to it!' But when the world is changing at warp speed, and every setback feels like a punch to the gut, it's no wonder we end up feeling lost, guilty and unsure of what comes next.

If you've picked up this book, you're most likely already feeling some level of uncertainty about your career and its future. There's an itch, a feeling of emptiness or dissatisfaction that you can't seem to shake off, and you know it's not just a phase. You've lost the love for what you do and don't quite know how to get it back. As I started to delve deeper into the world of job dissatisfaction, researching and processing the stories people were sharing with me, I realised that I too had experienced a career comedown – I just didn't know it at the time.

I spent seven years working in the advertising industry with the clear goal of working on purpose-led storytelling. But, as I devoted more and more time, effort and skill to my career, I was consistently met with overbearing workloads, a lack of clear boundaries, long working hours for salaries that didn't match, and a career trajectory that wasn't aligning with my skills and certainly wasn't bringing me consistent joy. I wasn't doing meaningful work; I'd become an email-pusher, a problem-firefighter and a manager of emotions. I hadn't signed up for that, so I would leave a company and take another role that promised to be different. Every role I moved to failed to meet my aspirations and left me feeling frazzled, unappreciated, overworked and questioning just how long I could keep going. Towards the end of my full-time career in advertising, I remember saying to myself before signing a new contract for yet another job, 'If I can't make it work

WHAT IS CAREER COMEDOWN?

here, I think I have to tap out of the industry altogether.' Three months later and I had handed in my resignation at my probation performance review.

I share all of this because I've been there. I've persevered with a career long after I'd realised it was not what it had been cracked up to be. I've worked longer and lonelier hours, even as I saw the returns diminishing, and I've come out the other side. It wasn't necessarily just the fault of my industry or my employer, but rather a mismatch between what I wanted to do, what I knew I could do and what I was doing.

The truth is many people feel career comedown but don't know how to come to terms with walking away from something in which they've invested so much of themselves. Especially when, superficially, things don't seem that bad: the pay is okay, the job is prestigious, or the company has promised progression. This is the *sunk cost fallacy*. It's that sneaky voice in your head telling you that since you've already spent so much time, money or emotional energy on something, you *have* to stick with it. But here's the thing: for me, the unhappiness eventually outweighed the fear of making a change. So, I took the plunge and turned my side hustle of helping people in their professional lives – something I loved doing as a passion project – into my full-time gig. Now, I'm not saying quitting is the answer for everyone, but taking an honest look at your future happiness (and not just the past investment) is always the first step when you're staring down a situation that's just not working for you anymore.

Aside from feeling trapped by their own past efforts, the other thing that often came up in the conversations I was having was that people felt like there was a lack of clarity on what should come next. Ultimately, this lack of clarity led to inaction, which in turn only caused more frustration. Career comedowns may be everywhere, but it seems no one knows what to do about them.

Here are some things I often heard when conducting interviews for this book:

- The culture will never change – can I keep going?
- I can't reach my life milestones – how do I make more money?
- There's no progression that feels appealing to me.
- The payoff doesn't feel worth it.
- I've never explored anything else.
- Is it too late to change?
- I don't have the energy to start from the bottom.
- I don't want to throw all my hard work out the window.
- I have commitments that rely on this salary.
- What will other people think or say about me?
- Is the grass even greener?

People talked to me about their problems in different industries using different words, but ultimately it all boiled down to five key areas . . .

1. Work Just Isn't Working

For years I've read article after article about how millennials and Gen-Z are impatient, disloyal, job-hopping workers who demand too much and work too little. *Newsweek* described Gen-Z as 'toxic for the workplace'[1] and the BBC labelled them as 'The Workers Who Want It All', not too dissimilar to the rhetoric of millennials when they entered the workforce.[2] But as I reflect on the numerous weekly conversations I'd had with my community over the past eight

WHAT IS CAREER COMEDOWN?

years and the insights I'd been gathering whilst writing this book, I realised the issue wasn't loyalty but that as a collective, employees and freelancers both have lost trust in the businesses they work for.

People are exhausted with overbearing workloads, budget cuts, layoffs, flexibility backtracks, office politics, zero job security and being forced to do more with less. There's a consistent feeling that businesses don't value or respect their employees' contributions, and hardworking employees are more likely to be rewarded with additional workload than a salary increase. It will come as no surprise that burnout is on the rise worldwide, with Gen-Z, millennials and women of all ages being most affected due to workplace stress. We all witnessed the great resignation post-pandemic, but now we're experiencing The Great Gloom – a collective sadness and lack of hope in relation to our futures, driven by various factors such as economic instability, climate change, social and political divisions, and mental health crises, with many people, particularly younger generations, feeling overwhelmed by the challenges of the modern world and the uncertain future.

According to a Harvard University study, Gen-Z and millennials tallied the lowest life-satisfaction scores across all age groups, and it was workplace experiences driving this dissatisfaction.[3] Reasons given varied from the inability to strike a work-life balance, not being able to take agreed holiday leave, not having strong support systems or not feeling challenged in their day-to-day role. These generations have only been working for fifteen years or less, and they are already struggling to stay afloat as the hustle and grind have become inescapable. We are over-connected and glued to work more than we ever have been. An already steady stream of emails is now punctuated by constant direct messaging through apps like Slack, and an out-of-office response is no longer accepted as a reason to not reply. Syreeta Brown, chief people officer for Virgin Money UK, told *Business Post*, 'It's not that there is more stress per se since Covid, but the nature has changed. All jobs are "always on" now, and there is an expectation that your diary can be filled up by others if they can find a gap. Stepping away from your laptop can feel mutinous.'[4]

Because this 'always on' culture has come coupled with increased uncertainty, people are nervous about setting clear boundaries and communicating their needs – instead they find themselves trapped and drowning in a never-ending cycle of unhappy work.

2. I Can't Afford To Follow My Passions

I couldn't write this book without acknowledging the impact a financial downturn can have on our career trajectory. For many people, the risk associated with pursuing a career they're truly passionate about, or taking the plunge and trying something new, is perceived to be not worth the financial stress. Many would, understandably, prefer to take jobs they can rely on to pay the bills, prioritising security over career ambitions.

I have met aspiring mothers who stay in jobs longer than they want to because they rely on maternity pay to keep them going. I know freelancers who have had to return to full-time employment because they couldn't sustain unpredictable workloads, contracts disappearing or ever longer payment terms. I've spoken to people who know they're being underpaid in their current role but fear looking elsewhere when they see cutbacks happening on a wide scale. The costs associated with housing, childcare, food and fuel have all skyrocketed, to the point where even those who are working salaried jobs in traditionally well-paid professions are feeling the pinch – according to the Office for National Statistics' latest survey, nearly half of those who earn a salary of more than

£50,000 claim they're needing to cut back on electricity and gas as the cost-of-living crisis grows.[5]

The anxiety around money is intense and, unsurprisingly, many people are finding reaching the life milestones previous generations reached at the same age – marriage, having children, buying a home – to be impossible. The lack of freedom and constant money worries mean that people are deprioritising what they really want to be doing for whatever keeps them out of debt.

3. I Chased Career Success Over Career Joy

Go to school, do well in your exams, get your qualifications, secure a job, push for every promotion and eventually it will pay off. This is generally the narrative we've been passed down, but at any point in our lives do we question if that's what we actually want? Over the last year I've spoken to many people who have confessed that the rat race is simply not for them. This revelation mainly came from people who have spent the first decade of their career moving from one level to the next, putting in the hours, securing the salary increases and reaching the leadership positions they always wanted, only to find themselves asking, *Is this it?*

On reflection, many of these people realised that they'd confused being good at something with being fulfilled by something. It's clear, now, that they've been living out a career fantasy placed on them by family, friends and societal norms, rather than one matching their own values. Chasing promotions and opportunities had brought them validation, but they had never consciously reflected on what a happy career would actually look like for them and instead mindlessly adhered to someone else's vision of success.

That was the case for Sarah in Manchester who, after spending nine years climbing the ladder and quickly achieving success, influence and a six-figure salary, realised she had been chasing an empty dream: 'It was impossible to unsee the industry flaws. My values had never been about making money, but I was on autopilot.' During our interview, Sarah shared that there was a moment where it hit her that all she was doing was making rich people richer and, despite her leadership position, she couldn't share the wealth fairly with the people who earned it. Two weeks later she handed in her notice to pursue work that was more meaningful to her.

We're living through a period of pushback to decades of career messaging that said more is more. The 'Girlboss' movement started as a push for female empowerment but quickly morphed into a pinkwashed hyper-capitalist mantra which became shorthand for working endless hours and blurring personal and professional boundaries. Meanwhile, men are still being told that pursuing career success over personal fulfilment is key to successful masculinity. So, it feels like now is a good time to question if sacrificing time with our loved ones and always feeling stressed over something that doesn't bring us joy is what we really want? There's been much discussion around 'Can we have it all?' over the years, but I think the debate should actually be, 'Do we really want it all anymore?'

4. I Chose The Wrong Path

'Find your dream job and you'll never work a day in your life,' they said. Growing up in the 2000s this was plastered on mugs, t-shirts and Etsy crochet cushions. But how true is it really? There are a million articles on how to find a dream job but very few on what to do when the dream job you've chased for years is in fact an utter disappointment. If you're having a career comedown because the thing you picked at school aged sixteen now no longer

WHAT IS CAREER COMEDOWN?

serves you fifteen years later, please know this is normal. We fantasise about careers we've never tried, only to feel like it's our fault when the reality doesn't match up with the vision in our heads. When you're young, being a doctor and saving lives feels like a dream job, but there is nothing dreamy about twenty-four-hour shifts and being severely underpaid.

We need to accept that our 'dream jobs' have often been intensely romanticised. In our minds, nothing goes wrong, everything is perfect and there are no barriers along the way. At no point, when fantasising about our future careers, do we stop to ask, *But what if I don't like it?* I spoke to life coach Gemma Perlin, who has found that many of her clients feel trapped in their careers, as though they're on a train and they have to stay put until the final destination. She believes part of the problem lies in the way we talk about career change, as if it's a loss. The phrase 'They're walking away from their career' is misleading. I prefer to say: 'They're not walking away . . . they're walking closer to who they really are.'

As humans, we are changing all the time, so it's inevitable that our interests, expectations and work needs will change alongside us, too. Yes, you may have picked a career, invested years in it and even seen some positive results, but that still doesn't mean you have to stay in it forever. You chose one of many paths and you can choose again.

You only have one life, so it's important to truly understand what it is that you want from your career. Maybe you really do care about money more than you once thought? Or perhaps, owning your time is the most important thing to you? The personal audit in the next chapter will encourage you to think about the things you want to unlearn, prioritise and carry into your everyday working life.

5. People Are Experiencing 'Careout'

One thing has become very apparent since writing this book is that there is a wave of people, particularly women, who are experiencing something I'm going to label as 'Careout'. Careout is the emotional and physical exhaustion that arises when you have spent years prioritising others' needs, smoothing over tension and doing what's 'right' for everyone else until there's nothing left to give. Careout isn't sudden. It builds slowly, almost invisibly, through years of compromise and quiet endurance. It's what happens when *care*, once a strength and source of connection, becomes a form of self-erasure. Many women reach careout in their thirties and forties, after a decade or more of being the reliable one, the understanding one, the one who keeps everyone else's worlds running. It's not just workplace burnout, it's a deeper, more personal depletion caused by the cultural expectation that women should be endlessly accommodating, empathic and available. As one woman described it to me, 'All my life I try to do the right thing and I don't do what I want to do because I worry about hurting other people – and it's just draining'. It's more than tiredness. Careout is the cumulative effect of:

- **Chronic compromise** – saying yes when you want to say no.
- **Emotional labor** – carrying everyone else's burdens while ignoring your own.
- **Self-erasure** – losing track of your wants, needs and priorities.
- **Social expectation** – feeling pressure to be endlessly nurturing, accommodating and 'good'.

WHAT IS CAREER COMEDOWN?

Careout is not about selfishness. It's the body, mind and spirit telling you that you've been running on empty. It's the turning point where doing the right thing for others can no longer come at the expense of yourself – where caring for yourself finally becomes as important as caring for everyone else.

CHAPTER 2
THE AUDIT

'What have *you* got to complain about?' is one of those loaded questions that you'll most likely be presented with when the people around you see your situation as better than theirs. Whilst it can be a useful grounding tool, it also has the power to make you suppress your true feelings about your career. I like to call this 'gratitude guilt': feeling bad for wanting change because other people tell you to be grateful. As I've built my business over the last seven years and helped countless people get what they want from their working lives, I've discovered that regular self-reflection is essential to growing and maintaining a happy career.

Without true reflection, it's easy for us to spend our entire lives complaining about the same things, over and over again, without ever acting. In my first book, *F*ck Being Humble*, I observed how easy it can be to cling on to a situation even when you know you are hating every minute and it's no longer serving you. You feel like a broken record every time you're asked to give a work update and even though it might seem obvious to everyone else what you need to do, you still struggle to make changes. In this chapter, we will explore an audit approach that will help you to gain clarity on what it is you really want.

The Art Of Not Settling

Have you ever felt like you're in a relationship with your job? I know it might sound strange admitting it out loud, but the connection we have to our careers can often carry the same amount of pressure and expectation that we feel in our love lives. And just as with romantic relationships, the spark we have with our work can fizzle out. When love and relationship doctor of psychology Dr Tari Mack shared her top reasons why people settle in relationships, I found they were alarmingly similar to the reasons we stay in work situations that don't serve us:[1]

1. You are afraid you won't find someone else.
2. They tick some boxes, but not all of them.
3. Your gut intuition is often trying to tell you that this is not the relationship for you.
4. You are afraid of hurting the someone if you leave, so you stay.
5. You wonder if you're settling and often fantasise about leaving.
6. You feel unhappy, unfulfilled or disconnected.
7. You don't feel emotionally safe.
8. You continue to tolerate bad behaviour.
9. You feel you are the only one putting in effort.

In Bevy Smith's TED talk, *How to Discover Your Authentic Self – at Any Age*, she shares her most essential life lessons, including this on settling: 'Settling is a really sinister thing. It will keep you up at night tossing and turning, trying to figure out why and trying to answer that age-old question: "Is that all there is?"

Personally, I don't have time for that, because the only time I want to be kept up all night long tossing and turning is when I'm in the company of a fine-ass man.'[2]

Aside from this being one of the most iconic lines to be dropped on the TED conference stage, this tossing and turning feeling is one that we can all relate to. She goes on to explain that having an intentional mindset to never settle means that she doesn't second-guess her decisions or worry about the future because she's firmly rooted in the present. Sounds nice, doesn't it? She wraps up the speech by saying, 'It took me fifty-five years to get here. So, Chris Rock, you're right. I'm a late bloomer. And that's OK. Because I'm right on time, Because it gets greater later.' When I first watched this speech, I remember smiling, frantically writing down every word in my iPhone notes and being uplifted by her infectious 'I-am-who-I-am' energy. But what I didn't expect was to keep coming back to those final words – 'It gets greater later.' We rarely hear this sentiment, especially in popular culture, but actually, it is the underpinning of this book. I want you to know that it's not all downhill from here just because you picked a route that you don't love, and there is an ending to your story where things get greater later.

Your Career Bucket List

For some strange reason, people often don't think about, let alone action, a bucket list until they hit the age of forty. A bucket list is a list of the experiences or achievements that a person hopes to have or accomplish during their lifetime, so isn't it better to start thinking about it sooner rather than later? Popular items normally include things like swimming the Great Barrier Reef or skydiving, but I think it's also a useful tool for designing the kind of career and working life we'd like. It's very easy to brush off our aspirations as unrealistic or unattainable, but I wish someone had told me that all my career goals would stay fictional if I didn't admit they were what I wanted and took the first small steps towards them. Just because you're from a small town, or you'd be the first person in your community to achieve something, doesn't mean you can't do it. Having dreams in our careers is the thing that keeps us going through the tough times, so before we go into your career audit, I want you to think about what you'd add to your career bucket list without worrying about how, when or if you'll get there. Here are a few examples that might spark some thoughts:

- I want to work and live in another country.
- I'd love to publish a book.
- I'd love to win an award.
- I'd love to become a mentor.
- I'd love to work remotely for twelve months.
- I'd love to launch my own art show.
- I'd love to have a successful podcast.
- I'd love to public speak in front of thousands of people.
- I'd love to have my own TV show.
- I'd love to be a stunt woman.
- I'd love to travel the world reviewing hotels.
- I'd love to save people's lives.

Some items on this list might seem a bit mundane to some, but you can and should go as big as you like when you're coming up with yours. The best part of a dream bucket list is that there are no rules!

THE AUDIT

What If You Don't Know What You Want?

I couldn't write this chapter without acknowledging the large percentage of people who might be reading this book because they don't actually know what they want their five-, ten- or twenty-year plan to be (spoiler alert: not many of us do!). According to *The Decision Dilemma* global study carried out by Oracle in 2023, 86 per cent of people feel information overload is making both personal and professional decisions more challenging, and 74 per cent of people say the number of decisions they make every day has increased ten times over the last three years.[3] So, if you're feeling unsure on where to go, you're not alone! This lack of clarity can be suffocating, especially when it feels like the people around you are forever flaunting how they've got everything worked out in your face. You know, the people who refer to every decision they make as working towards their 'masterplan' or those who ask you, 'So, what's your big plan for the year?' every single time you see them. Honestly, I can't help but laugh when this happens to me. Sorry to disappoint you, Barbara, but the only thing I'm consistently planning is what I'm going to watch on TV every night after a long day of work.

When you're in this place, any discussions about the future can feel triggering, because you feel like you should have cracked what you want to spend the rest of your life doing by now. But that is fundamentally not true. You might have grown up with parents or teachers saying, 'You might enjoy it, but where's it going to take you?' (and trust me, as a child who loved drawing with charcoal at school, I know how external doubts can dim your excitement), but there is so much value in pursuing your genuine interests, even if there isn't a concrete end goal in sight. So, instead of obsessing over the daunting question of 'What do I want to do with the rest of my life?', what if you asked yourself, 'What do I feel inspired to explore more deeply at *this* point in my life?' This question was shared as a tweet from author and wellbeing specialist Cory Muscara, who explained that reframing the question in this way 'removes the pressure to plan your life in one moment, and trains you to honour the ever-changing truth of your being'. Our need to have everything perfectly mapped out, with a clear financial trajectory and progression plan, often steers us away from the things we actually want to do in the present moment.

And if you are still reading this thinking, 'But I don't even know what I want to do in the present moment' (because, let's be honest, this can be a very real feeling), I want you to do a different activity – Field Notes. I first read about this concept when I picked up the book *Tiny Experiments* by Anne-Laure Le Cunff, a brilliant read on how to live freely in a goal-obsessed world.[4] I discovered the book when I was going through an in-between phase of my life and career and felt like I was stuck in the mud. Nothing was motivating me or able to capture my attention – even my vision board felt boring. So, as I dived into the book with little hope it would change my current state, I was instructed by the author to act like an anthropologist and make 'field notes' capturing my thoughts and feelings on my phone as they happened in real time. Your field notes can consist of anything, but the author recommends splitting it into categories like:

- **Insights:** Your moments of curiosity, random thoughts, new ideas and questions that spark your interests.
- **Energy:** Your shifts in energy levels through the day, as well as what gives you energy or drains your energy.
- **Mood:** Your emotions during or after an experience, whether it's a meeting, a workout or a podcast.

- **Encounters:** Your social interactions and any insights or feelings that arose from them.

The point of this is to capture what you are and are not drawn to. As the author explains: 'Field notes offer a way to become an active observer and to discover the interesting patterns in your life. Pay attention to invisible gaps and curiosity attractors. When you take a step back to consider a typical day of your life, do you feel like something is missing? Do you feel a yearning towards something different?' I spent four days writing everything I experienced, from rude confrontations with taxi drivers to films I watched that made me cry. Doing so not only made me feel more present and aware of my surroundings, but actually prompted me to look forward to making my next entry and seeing where my curiosity was guiding me. They weren't full of any wildly inspiring epiphanies or career-changing reflections, but as I sat through reading my field notes, I started to see patterns emerging which allowed me to reconnect with myself and my preferences.

What Does Wealth Really Mean To You?

When we think about the word wealth, our minds will naturally go to money – or lack thereof. If like me you're a reality TV lover, you might picture some of the ridiculous items you've seen people invest in on shows, like $4.5 million gold-plated toilets, $100,000 crystal-encrusted dog collars or my personal favourite . . . when Kyle Richards from *The Real Housewives of Beverly Hills* showed off a diamond-studded horse that she'd bought for an event. These extreme examples of wealth are what I and many others grew up watching and which have, in many ways, influenced our perception of what wealth is.

However, wealth comes in a lot of different forms. Some people are born into generational wealth, whilst others work hard to build their financial security for themselves. Then there are those who don't define their wealth by their bank balance or anything material but rather by what they have in abundance. Wealth is also being healthy, feeling safe and having the freedom to spend time with the people you care about. As we get older, we come to realise that our quality of life is not just defined by a number in our bank account but by how we experience our daily lives.

In writing this book, I realised that there are many people who are willing to make do with less income if it means keeping their time as their own. I know it might sound counterintuitive, especially when we're so conditioned to chase bigger paycheques, but what's the point of making millions of pounds if you don't have the time or capacity to actually enjoy it? There's a Chinese proverb that says that whilst an inch of time is worth an inch of gold, you cannot buy an inch of time with an inch of gold. One hundred per cent of the time you spend accumulating wealth is time you'll never get back. So, if all you do is work, no matter what your effective wage is, in terms of time and freedom you are poor. I say all of this, not because chasing money is a bad thing, but to inspire you to reflect on what 'wealth' really means to you.

Time To Self-Reflect

The purpose of this book is to help you to evaluate your present, so you're not robbing yourself of the future you deserve. The truth is most people don't reflect enough on their situations and their needs because they don't know the right questions to be asking themselves. So, I've carefully curated a list of questions that are going to help you with identifying your preferences that can later be turned into tangible actions.

Your current situation

Let's start with how you're feeling right now about your current situation. These questions are included to help you gain clarity on what is and is not working for you – the more honesty and detail you bring to them, the more helpful they will be.

- What do you place importance on?
- What do you currently do that you excel at?
- What gives you joy, a sense of satisfaction and energy?
- What things drain and deplete you?
- If you were to tell me about the journey you're going on, what would it look, sound and feel like?
- If you were independently wealthy, what would still make you come to work?

Your wants

For these questions, I want you to think about your ambitions and what you'd do if you had fewer obstacles in your life. Don't worry about how you will get there, just allow yourself the time to reflect honestly.

- What do you want for yourself?
- If you didn't consider other people's needs, what would you prioritise?
- What would you need to do to make your job more meaningful or inspirational?

- When you think of your ideal position, how does it differ from now?

Your future

For this section I want you to think about your future self and the decisions you will need to make to get you closer to where you want to be.

- How much worse does it need to get before you choose something different?
- What can you eliminate in your life to get you closer to what you want?
- What do you need to add to your life?
- How can you begin to fill the gap from where you are to where you want to be?

The trade-off

Now some of you might have answered these questions optimistically with excitement, but others might be thinking, 'This is all great, but you can't do a pick-and-mix of all my ideal outcomes and think it will just happen.' And to anyone thinking that, I agree. The reality is we all have to make trade-offs somewhere. I love my job and would go as far as to say I've built my dream career. BUT dream jobs still have downsides. I don't love sending invoices and chasing my clients to pay me or doing all of my own social media content creation, but something I actively chose was to not build a team. Why? Because one of my values is freedom, and when I dreamt up my ideal day it didn't involve managing people. Does that mean I have to do more admin tasks than I'd like sometimes? Yes, it does, but it also means

THE AUDIT

I spend the rest of my time focusing on the tasks I really do love, and I can take a six-month break whenever I want with no consequences (providing I have enough money in my bank account).

So now this is where we play a game of Would You Rather? and no, I'm not going to ask you if you'd rather work an overtime shift with your annoying boss or spend a full day with your mother-in-law. I want you to get real and decide what you're going to prioritise or de-prioritise for your next chapter. It's time to start thinking about what your non-negotiables are. When we get down to the nitty gritty, what is it that you are willing to tolerate and what are you not? What do you want vs what do you need? Is the security of a paycheque better than working for yourself? Is flexible working more important than climbing the ladder? You might change your answers as you work through this book but start thinking about them now and you'll have the opportunity to re-reflect towards the end.

Prompts to consider:

1. **Salary:** How much money is *really* enough?
2. **Your location:** What do you need from your surroundings?
3. **Career progression:** What is your ideal title, role and responsibilities?
4. **Flexible working:** Do you need it or is it something you can live without?
5. **Working alone or working with others:** Can you self-initiate or do you like being part of a team?

You'll most likely have other non-negotiables to add to your list, so tailor this until it feels right for what you need. The point of this section is to be honest with yourself and to build a criterion that specifically works for you.

Pick A Card

Now you've completed your career audit questions, we're going to dive into three options you can choose from to get closer to the career you want.

When I first observed career comedown amongst my friends, it was clear that whilst they could all identify that they were feeling it, they had no idea what they could do to solve it. Everyone kept telling me that it feels too hard, too risky or too late in the game to be mixing things up. The truth is the older we get the more comfortable with the status quo we become, and our risk-taking mindset can regress quite significantly. Until now, you might have felt that curing your career comedown was impossible. But I want you to know you do have the power to design a new path and follow it. I'm going to show you how to move from a 'how-did-I-get-this-so-wrong' mindset to an 'I-have-more-options-than-I-realised' outlook, and how you can choose a plan that works for you.

Whatever brought you to this point, you ultimately have three options:

Option 1 – Stick: Stay with your current career but mould it to reflect your current needs. Stick is for anyone who is not ready to change paths or still loves the core of what they do but feels as though they've lost their way. This is for those looking to reset boundaries, take back control of their career and shape it into something that makes sense for where they are now. It's about making considered changes and falling back in love with what set you on this path in the first place.

THE AUDIT

Option 2 – Twist: This option is for those looking to reinvent themselves, start again, pursue a dream or try something new – at any stage in their career. Whether you've decided life is too short or have just realised that the path you chose many moons ago is not the one for you, you're ready to leap into a new direction and follow your current calling.

Option 3 – Tap Out: The final option is to tap out of work being your sole identity. You want to decentre your career and have decided it's no longer the key signifier for a successful life. You're ready to consider a world beyond the question, 'So what do you do?' This is for anyone who is sick of the hustle and wants to find a low-maintenance career that gives them the time to enjoy the rest of the joys in their life.

Now we've outlined the three cards in your hand, let's dive into your first option: Stick.

CHAPTER 3
STICK

WHAT TO DO WHEN YOU'RE NOT READY TO LEAVE IT BEHIND

If you've found yourself in a position where you're no longer enjoying your day job, then I'm sure you've already been told to quit and start something new. Whilst it might be tempting and, in some ways, easier to jump ship, there's likely still something in you that's not ready to give up on your specific career path just yet. It's not about the money or your pride but rather a genuine desire to stay in the industry because you feel in your core that you still have so much to offer and that there are many things you'd still love to achieve. Or maybe it's not feasible for you to move on right now, and sticking things out is the right choice for the season you're in. If this is you, then starting over isn't the solution you're looking for. Instead, the focus should be moulding your job to your current needs or at least trying to find more joy in it. It's about taking back control so you can reignite the spark that set you on this path in the first place. In this chapter we're going to explore how you can stick in your chosen role or industry, and at the same time make changes that will allow you to have a happier work relationship and not look back in regret.

Choosing To Stick

Let's be real, you're most likely feeling some anger, frustration and irritation about your current situation. From my research and the many conversations I've had with those who are unhappy, the key factors that are causing people to feel discontentment are the following:

You're bored at work

Maybe you don't need to quit, you're just unbelievably bored? Every day feels like a struggle to show up and act like you care. You're dragging yourself through the day, stuck in a loop of yawns, glazed-over eyes and an ever-growing 'meh' about everything. Days feel unbearably long, tasks feel mind-numbingly dull and you've not felt that get-up-out-of-bed energy for an alarmingly long time.

Interestingly, being bored isn't always just a passing feeling and this type actually has a name: 'boreout'. Whilst burnout happens when we're overwhelmed and overworked, boreout is the opposite. It's what happens when work feels unchallenging, lacking in purpose and mentally unstimulating – which can be just as draining. Dr Mandy Lehto, an executive coach and host of the podcast *Enough*, explains in an article for *Happiful* magazine that boredom at work often stems from feeling powerless or lacking agency: 'It's a feeling of being resigned to a situation that isn't fully challenging you,' she says.[1] When that happens, our energy drops, motivation fades and we're left feeling disengaged and depleted.

The people around you

You've probably heard the saying, 'People don't leave jobs, they leave bosses.' According to the 'Horrible Bosses: A survey of the American Workforce', 82 per cent of people across 10 industries say they would quit their job due to bad managers,[2] whilst HR News have reported that 67 per cent of workers in the UK are said to have quit or considered quitting due to their boss.[3] And it's not always the boss, maybe it's the cliques, the gossip, the lack of trust or the feeling that you just don't belong. Even learned behaviours such as how people treat one another, what gets rewarded and what gets ignored, can make you question whether you want to keep showing up. If you're self-employed, it doesn't necessarily get easier – 'client dread' is real. Just the thought of certain names popping up in your inbox can drain your energy and zap your motivation. The tough part? In some industries, these people-problems follow you wherever you go, so even if you move jobs, you know you'll still be met with much of the same.

Your physical work environment

Working in a soul-destroying environment? Got a commute that takes up far too much of your day? Finding that your workstation is not conducive to doing your best work? Or that it's interfering with your life responsibilities? These are all things that have been highlighted to me during my interviews as reasons people were feeling conflicted about their job and they are factors that can hinder us from enjoying our work. Since the pandemic, conversations around where and how we work have become increasingly prominent. For some of you, the thought of returning to office life and giving up your finely tuned at-home routine sparks nothing but frustration. For others, the make-shift desk setup has long lost its charm, and you're craving real human connection. Then there are those of you whose work environment never moved at all, it just got worse due to budget cuts, overcrowding and limited resources.

The truth is, just like the homes we live in, our work environments shape how we feel, how we think and how well we show up. When the space around us isn't working, it's no surprise that everything else starts to feel off, too. A cluttered or chaotic environment can leave us feeling overwhelmed, while a sterile, impersonal one can chip away at our sense of connection and motivation. Over time, those small, physical discomforts add up until they start affecting how we feel about our entire job. When your environment doesn't support your needs, it's not just frustrating, it's exhausting, and it becomes one more reason you start counting down the minutes until the workday ends.

Your progression is unpredictable

Progression in every industry can look different, but depending on the company's performance, the industry trends and the decision-makers calling the shots, your journey can often feel like it's in the hands of other people. I've had endless conversations with people who attend my events expressing their disappointment that promotion and pay freezes are stopping them from climbing the ladder, whilst others have quietly settled into workplaces that stopped supporting them years ago, hoping something might eventually change. And the numbers back it up, a study by IRIS Software Group and YouGov found that nearly half of employees (47 per cent) can't see a clear path to progression.[4] Even more concerning? Around 68 per cent of UK workers say their career growth has been delayed thanks to a lack of support from their managers and HR teams.[5]

One of the biggest reasons a lack of progression feels so frustrating is because it challenges a core human need: growth. Most of us want to feel like we're evolving, learning and moving towards something bigger. When that momentum stalls, it's not just about missing out on a new title or pay bump, it's about losing a sense of purpose (and regularly asking yourself, 'What's the effing point?!). We start to question our value, our potential and sometimes even our decision to stay in the role. Without visible signs of progress, it's easy to feel stuck and disconnected from the very work we once cared about.

Lacking freedom and autonomy

You've put in the hours, shown your commitment, built up experience and yet you're still being second-guessed, micromanaged or kept on a tight leash. It's frustrating when you've worked so hard to prove yourself, but the freedom to make decisions or lead projects just isn't there. Maybe it's a controlling manager, rigid processes or clients that think they can do your job better. Whatever the reason, it leaves you feeling stuck, like you're just a pair of hands rather than a capable, thinking professional. And over time, that lack of trust starts to chip away at your confidence. You hesitate more. You stop sharing new ideas. You lose that spark you once brought to the role.

Autonomy isn't just a nice-to-have, it's one of the key drivers of job satisfaction and when you don't have it even the most exciting work can feel like a chore. What makes it even harder is knowing how much more you could give, if only you were trusted to do things your way. You can see the potential for better outcomes, smoother processes, more creative solutions, but your hands are tied. Instead of being empowered to lead, you're stuck waiting for approvals, stuck in meetings that go nowhere, stuck defending decisions that should be yours to make. That inner drive you once had starts to fade, and showing up becomes more about surviving the day than doing work you're proud of. It's not about ego, it's about wanting to be treated like a professional who's earned the right to be trusted.

Conflicting workplace policies

There's a quiet kind of tension that builds when you're working for or with company whose values don't quite match your own. It might not hit all at once, sometimes it starts small. A decision that feels off. A policy that seems unfair. A leadership comment that doesn't sit right. But over time, those moments stack up, and suddenly you're left questioning not just the work you're doing, but why you're doing it and who you're doing it for. Maybe the company talks a big game about mental health but punishes people for setting boundaries. Maybe they preach diversity and inclusion, but the boardroom still looks the same as it did ten years ago. Or maybe it's the way your team is pushed to hit targets, no matter the human cost. It's exhausting trying to do your job well whilst also carrying the emotional weight of pretending you're okay with things that go against your core values. You feel torn between your career and your conscience, and that internal conflict chips away at your motivation, your trust in leadership, and sometimes, even your self-worth. Because it's hard to feel proud of your work when deep down, something about the way it's being done doesn't feel right. And when you're spending so much of your time and energy at a place that doesn't align with who you are, that misalignment follows you home, lingers in the back of your mind, and makes it harder and harder to show up as your best self. At some point, it's not just about a job anymore, it's about the kind of person you want to be.

You don't feel valued

Being consistently overlooked doesn't just affect your motivation, it warps your entire outlook. You hit your targets, you show up with a positive attitude, you're the one people can count on. You collaborate, support others, bring ideas to the table, and genuinely want the team to thrive. But despite all that, the praise never comes. Your effort goes unacknowledged, your wins get brushed under the rug or, worse, claimed by someone else. You go from being someone who gives their all to someone who's just trying to make it to Friday. It's a slow erosion of your self-belief, and it can leave you questioning whether the problem is you, when deep down, you know it isn't. It's hard to stay hopeful when your efforts are constantly being hijacked, dismissed or ignored. And when recognition is only handed out to the loudest or most politically savvy voices in the room, it becomes harder and harder to keep showing up with heart. Because at the end of the day, everyone wants to feel seen. Everyone wants to feel like they matter. And when you're constantly made to feel like a background character in your own career story, eventually something inside you starts to shut down.

Whatever is causing your career comedown, you've got to be willing to start afresh or put your emotions on hold if you're choosing to stick. I say this because I've watched too many people in my life have a 'one-foot-in one-foot-out' mindset which looks and sounds like this:

- Convincing yourself you shouldn't have bothered when the first speedbump comes along instead of working through the problem.
- Saying things like, 'How unexpected' in a high-pitched passive-aggressive tone, when someone does something you don't like.
- Repeatedly saying, 'I'm giving xxx time until I ditch it altogether.'
- Waiting for the stars to align and things to change without changing how you approach situations.
- Assuming people are mind readers and should know you want something, even though you've not told them.
- Insisting that you're open but then dismissing suggestions from others.

You say you're giving it another go, but what you're actually looking for is any misstep or obstacle to prove why the industry or role will always be the same. This is known as confirmation bias – the tendency to search for, interpret, favour and recall information in a way that supports one's prior beliefs. The reason you might do this is to protect yourself, because you're worried if you put all your eggs back in the same basket you'll look stupid if they end up disappointing you again. But here's the problem with this: whether you realise it or not, you'll only ever be half committed. In the back of your mind, you'll always be looking for a reason for why you should give up and that will get in the way of your potential growth. If you want to stick in your industry, I urge you to let go of old resentments and start with a clean slate. Choosing to stay is hard for many reasons, but once you've made that choice you owe it to yourself to give it everything you've got.

STICK

Good reasons to stick	Bad reasons to stick
You see potential where you are	You like the team away days and free drinks on a Friday
You have more ideas or things you want to action	You can stay in an environment where you don't have to have honest conversations, and keep tip toeing around what you really want
You're open to getting real, setting boundaries and communicating more	You're avoiding confrontation and don't want to look uncapable
You see ways that you can ask for help or work with others to support you	You can keep coasting and there is less disruption to your life
You're willing to change your patterns and behaviours	You assume everywhere will be the same so you shouldn't vere away from what you know

If you're choosing to stick, it's important that you do so on your own terms. Sure, it might mean having some tough conversations and stepping out of your comfort zone a bit, but you're doing it because you know it's all part of getting closer to what you really want down the road. Sometimes, making just a few small adjustments can turn things around faster than you'd expect, without needing to start over or invest time in something completely new.

That said, before we dive deeper into this chapter, I want to give you a heads-up: sticking with your career does also come with some challenges. For one, the outcome you're aiming for might not always be in your control. There could be times when your preferences just can't be met, or there are bigger systemic barriers that keep popping up, no matter how hard you push forward. This is not to say it's not worth trying, and if you have the capacity to, it's actually the thing I'd recommend. What I really want to emphasise is that if you're still feeling dissatisfied after trying the tips we're going to talk about, don't lose hope. A fulfilling career *is* out there for you. It might just take a bit more time or a different approach to get there. The following are three mindset shifts I need you to embrace if you are to seek out a better style of work for yourself.

Mindset shift 1: If you don't ask you don't get

I can't tell you how many times someone has come to me saying, 'I've tried everything.' And whilst I totally get the frustration behind that, I often think . . . *Have you really?* Here's the thing, most of us try everything we feel comfortable trying. We stick to what feels safe, and without realising it, avoid the actions that push us out of our comfort zones. Psychologist Leon Festinger, who developed the theory of cognitive dissonance, explained that we feel internal discomfort when our actions don't align with our goals. To ease that tension, we sometimes convince ourselves we've done all we can, even when we haven't. Saying, 'I've tried everything' can be a protective response, a way to soften the sting of things not going to plan. But real growth often begins when we gently challenge that story and ask, 'What haven't I tried because it feels uncomfortable or unfamiliar?' Sometimes, the next step isn't about doing more, it's about doing something different.

So, when someone says they've 'tried everything', I can almost always think of one thing they haven't. Often, the most frustrated people at work are the ones venting loudly at the pub but staying surprisingly quiet in one-to-ones with their manager. It's not that they don't have a voice, but they might not feel confident or empowered to use it where it actually matters. If that sounds familiar, maybe you've slipped into a bit of a 'what's the point?' mindset, especially if you've faced rejection or felt unheard in the past. That's totally human. But I want to gently remind you that your voice does matter. And using it is often the first step towards real change. You don't need to shout to be heard, you just need to believe you're worth being listened to. So, before you tell yourself you've done all you can, take a moment to check in honestly: have you really explored every option, even the uncomfortable ones? You can't control every outcome, but you can control your effort, your voice and how you show up. That's where momentum starts.

Mindset shift 2: Find rooms that respect you

For the first five to ten years of your career, proving your worth can feel like your primary focus. You're new in the game, you're learning on the go, you're discovering what you like and don't like and you're mostly looking for approval. They say jump and you say how high. That was definitely the case for me and many of my peers as we navigated the working world for the first time. Long hours, overcommitting and going above and beyond was the theme of my twenties; I did it all to build credibility and respect. But at what point do you move out of the 'earning your stripes' zone and into the 'I'm too qualified for this' realm?

This feeling is one that frequently came up in the interviews I conducted for this book. Many people reach their thirties and forties still feeling underappreciated and questioning why they're not working at the level they know they're capable of. One person told me that, despite working at her company for ten years, she still found herself buried in tasks that were no longer a good use of her time or the company's money, simply because she hadn't had the courage to remind her team that she'd outgrown those responsibilities. Her colleagues had become so used to her picking up these tasks that it became part of her work identity, and no one thought to offer her a hand or take them off her plate. A common thread across these conversations was that she hadn't changed her own actions to reflect her reputation and that's why she kept finding herself in situations where she didn't feel respected. It was her lack of self-advocacy, boundary-setting and clear communication that sent her in the same direction time and time again. If this sounds like you, I want you to know that you absolutely deserve to be in spaces where you're respected. But sadly (as some of you may have already experienced) the working world doesn't always reward you accordingly just because you deserve it. You have to advocate for yourself and assume that no one else will do it for you. You've got to be the one to set that standard for yourself. You've got to make decisions about what you're willing to accept and what you're not if you want to feel that sense of self-worth. You've earned your stripes, now it's time to own them.

Mindset shift 3: Accepting the limitations

A lot of our resentment about our chosen career comes from not fully accepting the limitations of the industry we're in. As I've got older, I've come to realise that the whole idea of 'having it all' is pretty much a myth. So when I asked you to do the trade-off activity in chapter 2, and really figure out what's most important to you, that was my way of reminding you that our jobs can't meet *every* need we have. Our expectations of dream-like careers are what got us to this point, so we have to be real with the choices we make if we want to stick to the same industry. As soon as I realised that my career couldn't and shouldn't meet all of my needs, I was able to make much more strategic career moves, and I want you to be able to do the same. For example, let's say what you really want is more time. That might mean narrowing your options, working seasonal jobs, earning less or adjusting your lifestyle expectations. The key is that you're making these choices consciously, knowing what you're gaining in return. It's all about finding balance and making decisions that align with what truly matters to you.

Now we've established why you might be sticking, and the mindset shifts you need to embrace to do so, let's start jumping into the practical ways you can keep moving forward in your chosen job or industry. Throughout this chapter we're going to look at how you can value yourself more in order to command more respect, authority and open up more opportunities. Then we'll explore how you can add more joy to your days and reduce that Sunday-night fear. And finally, we're going to do a deep dive into how you can adapt communication styles, build better relationships and set clear boundaries to transform your relationship to work.

Stop Playing Small

For the last eight years I have dedicated my days to helping people advocate for themselves. But one of the hardest things I've had to observe is incredible talent not getting what they deserve because they were playing too small. Cindy Gallop, one of my favourite marketing icons and all-round empowerment bosses, says, 'People value you at the value you are seen to put on yourself' and she's absolutely right.[6] From my experience, the people who tend to get what they want in their careers know their strengths, can speak about them confidently and set clear standards for how they want to work and be treated. That kind of clarity not only helps others understand your value, it also helps you protect your time and energy. When we don't do that, it's easy to overcommit, say yes when we mean no and feel quietly resentful.

When I worked full time, I used to be a serial job hopper. Every eighteen to twenty-four months, if I didn't feel like my value was being celebrated, I was out of there. But I only made that choice because my very first job after graduation was so toxic and confidence-shattering, I promised myself I'd never stick in a situation that made me feel worthless again. When you struggle with low self-esteem or feel inadequate, you are more likely to take on things you don't want to be doing, accept bad treatment or stay in environments you've outgrown. So, if you're reading this book knowing that you don't big yourself up as much as you should, now is the time to change things up. The more you self-reflect regularly and celebrate your positive steps of progress, the more your credibility grows. When we don't do this, we can easily trick ourselves or let other people make us feel we're not enough yet. But I need you to know that you are more than enough, you just need to spend more time reminding yourself you are. Before we get into examples on how you can celebrate yourself more, let's first reflect on some questions that help you to see your own value:

- What value do you bring to the table?
- How do people who value themselves act and behave?
- What changes might you need to make to get better at valuing yourself?

Proud moments folder

So, what does it look like to recognise your self-worth in real time? Well, if you've been to any of my workshops or talks, you'll have most likely heard me speak about the importance of having a folder on your laptop or your mobile phone called 'Proud Moments'. This was something I started as, like many of you, I was regularly overlooking my progress and letting my imposter syndrome drive the narrative that I wasn't worthy enough. When exciting opportunities came around, I would think of all the reasons I couldn't do something instead of drawing upon all the times I have succeeded. Now, whenever I do something I am proud of, happy with or didn't think was possible, I add it to my proud moments folder as evidence of my success.

For me, my folder consists of things like:

- Nice feedback I've received.
- Finally launching the thing I've banged on about for a year.
- Videos that I found difficult to share (and after 200 takes eventually shared).
- People sitting on my front row at events.
- Sitting on front rows of my friends' events.
- Screenshots of supportive texts from friends and family.
- Photos of my walks *reminding me why it's so important to take breaks*.
- Things I was scared to do.
- Things I'd put off doing.
- R & R days.
- Screenshots from my therapy sessions.

- Photos of my continuous journaling (I resisted it for years and then realised how much I enjoyed it).
- Connection requests following interesting meetings.
- Signing new contracts.

What's great about this is you start to build a visual archive of moments – a storyline of your successes, your courage and your motivation. It's been a game-changer for myself and many people in my network, but it's a particularly good activity to do if you're going through a career comedown. Seeing what you add to that folder will give you an indication of your internal motivators and it's a great way to explore how you measure success in private when other people aren't influencing you. This isn't just about knowing your worth and asking for it, it's about documenting what gives you that get-out-of-bed energy and working closer towards doing more of that.

Nurturing your self-worth

When I quit my job, it didn't take long for me to realise just how much I relied on external validation. I missed having managers or colleagues around to motivate me, give me a thumbs-up or throw some praise my way, especially when the world went into lockdown. But as I got further into my self-employed journey, one thing became super clear: I needed to learn how to validate myself instead of constantly waiting for someone else to do it. Whether you're working at a company or running your own business, this is a game changer. When I deliver talks, I can't always guarantee that people will communicate their enjoyment of the session with me, and although I used to struggle if I wasn't showered with praise, I decided I don't want my worth to be defined by other people. So, I took matters into my own hands and created criteria for myself, as a way to measure my performance that's totally independent of external feedback. Now when I do my job, I ask myself the following things:

- Did I enjoy myself?
- Did I offer something of value?
- Did I explain my thinking clearly?
- Did I feel proud of what I did?
- Did I handle things professionally?
- Did I respond to the brief as well as I could?
- Did I demonstrate confidence in myself?
- Would eighteen-year-old me be impressed?
- If I were to do it again, would I do it the same way?

These questions have had a huge impact on my confidence. Don't get me wrong, I'd be extremely grateful if you leave a written review on Amazon about how wonderful you think this book is or DM me to say how much you liked my recent talk, but if I don't hear from you, I've learned to stop self-sabotaging and doubting myself.

There are going to be times in your career where you don't receive the well-deserved validation you are looking for, but just because you don't receive it doesn't mean you have to get in a vicious cycle of taking on more so you can prove yourself all over again. As Brianne West says in her book *The Mountain Is You*: 'There's a difference between passionately committing to something and feeling obligated to outperform everyone else. One is healthy and the other is not.'[7] If you want to have a healthy work-life balance, you need to set boundaries that stop you from spiralling every time you don't receive validation from others.

Knowing your value is one thing but communicating that with confidence is what gets results. I spoke to Lisa O'Hare, who, after twenty years in her industry, took a voluntary redundancy and spent six months rethinking her next career move. She realised she no longer wanted to work with large corporates and aimed to cut down to a three-day workweek. When she found a great role advertised as full time (five days week), she had a choice: move on or mould it to suit her. She applied for the job but pitched herself as being able to fulfil the role over three days a week. She knew she could deliver high-quality results in fewer hours thanks to her experience. The value she brought made it a smart deal for both sides.

What I loved about this story was Lisa knew her value. She didn't let the job advert constraints limit her; she clearly communicated the business case and she scored a part-time job that worked on her terms. None of this would be possible if Lisa hadn't spent time reflecting on how brilliant an asset she was and how well she could do her job. So, this is your reminder: if you want to find a career that works on your terms, you need to start documenting and believing that you're worth the requests you put in for.

Cut the self-blaming and shaming

At the start of your career, when things go wrong you can often hold your hands up to you making a mistake and being a beginner. But something I've noticed in the interviews I conducted is how often people slip into self-deprecating talk. They're quick to point out their flaws or blame themselves for why their career hasn't gone the way they hoped. Whilst a bit of humility early on can help you avoid coming across as arrogant, there comes a point where that habit can start to hold you back. If you're aiming to be seen as capable, reliable, trustworthy or a leader in your space, it's important to shift out of the 'I'm such an idiot' mindset (even if you're saying it jokingly). Constant self-criticism, even in a light-hearted way, can make others question your confidence and abilities. You don't need to be perfect, but you do need to be able to back yourself up and avoid creating doubt around you.

When you come up against setbacks or challenges (and we all do), try shifting from PIG beliefs to SET beliefs. In cognitive behavioural therapy (CBT), PIG stands for Permanent, Internal and General. These are thought patterns that can make things feel overwhelming or hopeless, like believing a problem is all your fault, will last forever or affects everything. Instead, think SET: Specific, External and Temporary. This means recognising that the setback is about a particular situation, caused by something outside of you, and that it won't last forever. By adopting SET thinking, you give yourself room to see challenges in a more balanced way, with less self-blame and a greater sense of hope. It's a powerful way to break out of unhelpful patterns and move forward with confidence.

The reason I'm bringing this up is because the style you use can have a big impact on your mood, confidence and how you bounce back from difficulties. Learning to shift towards a more flexible, realistic and compassionate explanatory style, like seeing challenges as temporary and specific, can really help build resilience and a healthier mindset. Plus, it helps to position you more positively, which will garner you more respect from others – the ultimate goal.

PIG beliefs	SET beliefs
Permanent: A person with a permanent belief assumes that a negative event will continue indefinitely. They believe it will always be this way, or that it will stay the same for a long time.	**Specific:** The belief is focused on a particular situation or event rather than a general or pervasive characteristic.
Internal: An internal belief suggests that the negative event is their own fault. They see themselves as the source of the problem, even when there is external influence.	**External:** The cause is attributed to factors outside the individual's control, such as luck, circumstance, or others' actions.
General: A general belief implies that the negative event is a reflection of a larger pattern in their life. They believe that the negative event is a representation of their overall character or ability.	**Temporary:** The belief is seen as a short-term issue that can be changed or overcome, not a permanent fixture.

Build your hype crowd

When I reflect on the most important things that have helped me to build my confidence over the years and stopped me from devaluing myself, it's been the cheerleaders in my corner spurring me on. These people have been family members, my fiancé, friends, peers in my network and mentors. The relationships you have in your life will affect how you see yourself and what you are willing to accept. If your bosses, colleagues or clients leave you second-guessing your worth, it's time to focus on the relationships that *actually* make you feel good about yourself. From my experience you need two types of people: motivators and supporters.

Motivators are the ones who push you to get to the finish line, even when you're convinced it's not possible. They're usually mentors, or people a few steps ahead of you, who can drop some serious wisdom and give you those little nudges when you need them. These people don't take 'no' for an answer and are your go-to thinking partners when you need to talk through your next move. They've got your back, and they won't let you settle for less than you deserve.

Supporters, on the other hand, are your ride-or-die crew. These are the friends, family, or that one work bestie who shows up for you when you take the leap. They're there for the big moments, cheering you on from the front row, both literally and metaphorically, the ones who make you feel like you can take on the world, no matter what.

What both of these groups should have in common is they will reassure you with statements like:

- 'You're worth so much more than that.'
- 'They don't realise how lucky they are to have you.'
- 'One day, they will kick themselves for overlooking you.'
- 'They clearly don't know what they're talking about.'
- 'You don't need them as much as they need you.'

These positive words of affirmation are exactly what you need to hear if self-doubt plays a prominent part in your internal dialogue. Even if they are saying it because they love you or they care deeply about your wellbeing, take it, and don't question it. You need to balance out your negative thoughts with positive reinforcements from others who think you are brilliant, so there's a balanced argument in your head. These people aren't there to inflate your ego, they are there to show you that you're worth it, even if you can't see it yourself.

If you commit to everything we've just discussed, you can at least go to bed each night knowing that you showed up for yourself. The reason I wanted to start this section specifically exploring self-worth is because you can't level up in your career if you don't see the value you bring. Remember, you have to change your internal view of yourself if you want to positively influence how others see you.

Find More Joy

Now we've covered self-belief and knowing your worth to get what you want, let's start exploring how you can add more joy into your working life and get you out of that rut you're experiencing. At the start of this chapter, I explored how boredom, lack of progression, environments, relationships, lack of autonomy, conflicting policies and not feeling valued can also result in you feeling stuck in your career. In an ideal world these things would all be taken care of, but in reality they are going to ebb and flow into one another, so the more you can learn how to tackle them when they appear, the better. One of my favourite quotes on this topic is: 'You can't add more days to your life, but you can add more life to your days.' Rather than accepting that feeling of being trapped and hopeless, let's look at some practical ways you can find more joy in your current professional situation.

Break free from boredom

I can't tell you how many times I've felt bored in my career. It happened all the time when I worked for other people, and (surprise!) it still happens now, even though I work for myself. Boredom or 'boreout' is far more common than you might think, though it's rarely spoken about as doing so feels like outing yourself. You don't want to look uncommitted, you don't want to seem disengaged, and you definitely don't want to come across like you don't know what you want. I know, because I've worried about all three.

I remember having an honest conversation with a former boss about feeling totally uninspired by the projects I was assigned. I'd joined the company because of their big-name clients but found myself stuck with dull briefs and even duller tasks. It was even harder watching colleagues get assigned to the flashy, exciting stuff whilst I felt like I was stuck in the slow lane. After I expressed this to my boss, candidly, he took it on board and, a few months later, I got put on a job for a huge sports brand. It sounded exciting, until it wasn't. The work turned out to be just as repetitive, just in fancier packaging. No getting involved in the creative process, no change in environment, just sat at the same desk, staring at the same four walls. That experience taught me that when it comes to navigating boredom, you've got to get really specific. Chasing prestige or 'cool' things won't fix it. If the work itself doesn't change, the boredom won't either.

A really good starting point is asking yourself what top five emotions you feel in relation to your workload. Are words like 'uninspired', 'repetitive', 'isolated', 'dread' or 'irritated' coming to mind? If so, you're not alone. Once you've written down these words, I want you to write the emotions you want to feel when working and compare the two lists. By seeing these words plainly in writing, you can start to observe which responsibilities or opportunities might align with those feelings – if you want to feel 'brave' when working for example, then perhaps taking opportunities to present to clients might be something you'd like to integrate into your role. A couple of questions that might help you reflect on this are:

- If a dream project or responsibility were to land on your desk, what would you be doing?
- What do you definitely not want to be doing more of?
- Is this available currently in the business? Is it something you might have to initiate as a first? Is it something you explore outside of work?

Now we've identified what might spruce up your days, we need to think about how to tee up the conversation with colleagues or leaders. First things first, you need to make sure that you're killing it on the tasks you're already meant to be doing. I hear it time and time again from leaders, that employees are demanding more whilst underperforming on their current workload. Leaders need to feel like you've hit it out the park before they commit to putting you forward for something new so don't give them any reason to doubt you. If you're unsure about where you stand, you can always ask them this simple question: 'Are there any other things you'd like to see from me for this to be a great success in your eyes?' This will either prompt them to give you a list of things you need to try or confirm that you're already doing a great job. If the latter is the case, let's look at how you can bring up amending your role with your boss without 'outing' yourself.

> **Script**
>
> *As you know I've been working on [insert responsibilities] and the results have been really positive, which I'm really pleased about.*
>
> *Moving forward and as part of my progression, I'd really love to develop my skills in [insert skills] and I'd love to explore more variation in my daily schedule. Are there any opportunities for me to [insert specific tasks you'd like to do more of] across the business?*
>
> *Doing more of this would feel really exciting, and I believe would help me to develop skills that I can apply across other areas of the company.*

By expressing yourself in this way, you're not saying that you're miserable or you're drowning in boredom, but you are proactively signalling to your boss the areas you'd like to improve on with specific examples of what that could look like. The opening sentence reinforces you're a trusted employee that has proven themselves; the second paragraph provides the detail on what you'd like more of; and the final sentence highlights the benefit of why this person should help to make this happen or how it will help the overall company success.

TOP TIP: *Change can't always happen overnight. Yes, I know waiting is long but give the decision-makers space to digest your request and put a plan in place. It might not be as quick a process as you think, so make sure you ask about timelines and how soon this could happen.*

CAREER COMEDOWN

If you're self-employed, you probably know that boredom can hit differently, sometimes even harder, when you're the one calling the shots. You might've left your old job to follow your passion, only to find yourself doing tasks that don't exactly spark joy. And here's the truth: being your own boss doesn't mean you're in control of everything, and experiencing boredom doesn't mean you've permanently fallen out of love with your work. It might just mean the routine is wearing thin or that slow-moving clients are zapping your momentum. If you can't shake up your client work right now, try carving out a small pocket of time – maybe two or so hours a week – for something that's just for *you*. This could be during a lunch break, a quiet hour in the morning, or by saying no to something that's draining you. The goal isn't to overhaul your schedule but to spark that energy again. Keep it small and manageable, and something you can look forward to each time. Personally, I like to give myself one creative project per quarter. I write a little brief, set a deadline, and by the end of the year I've created things I'm genuinely proud of. No approvals, no budgets, just pure, red-tape-free creativity. It works wonders and has led me to working on things I might never have had land on my desk.

- Where in your week could you do personal work projects?
- What would you love to explore?
- What would you love to look back on in your year and feel proud of doing?
- What doesn't require too much energy or commitment to stay on top of?

Break the script

Instead of focusing on *what* you're doing, another way you could find more joy is to change *how* you're doing something. In their book *Power of Moments*, authors Dan and Chip Heath explore how we can create more powerful and memorable moments in our personal and professional lives.[8] According to them, '. . . the more routine something is in general, the less memorable it is.' They go on to explain how important it is to 'break the script' in our days and encourage readers to think about how this could be applied to their own lives – whether that's disrupting the format of a meeting, changing the way you respond to customers or adapting how you finish a project to make it feel more momentous.

A couple of examples included:

> **Hilton Lost Teddy Bear.** A family accidentally left their daughter's beloved teddy bear behind at a Hilton hotel. When the parents called, Hilton staff had already found the bear and went above and beyond. They returned it with photos showing the bear 'enjoying' his extended stay: lounging by the pool, getting a spa treatment, even helping out at the front desk. It was a small act with a big impact. By creating an unexpected, heartwarming experience, Hilton transformed a simple lost-and-found moment into a lasting memory, showing how small gestures can create powerful emotional connections.

> **Steve Jobs Held a Funeral for a Computer.** Steve Jobs, upon returning to Apple, held a symbolic funeral for the original Macintosh operating system OS9. The once iconic product had become outdated, and Jobs knew Apple needed a fresh start. Instead of quietly retiring it, he staged a dramatic farewell to mark the end of an era. This moment wasn't just

theatrical, it was strategic. By publicly letting go of the past, Jobs helped his team emotionally shift towards a new vision.

> **Personalised Classmate Notes.** In a high school classroom, a teacher recognised that many students go through school feeling unseen or underappreciated. To change that, she launched a simple yet powerful project: each student was asked to write a heartfelt, positive note about every single one of their classmates. The notes were compiled and delivered as personalised packets. Students said it was one of the most meaningful moments of their school life, showing how small acknowledgments can create powerful emotional impact.

I'm sharing these examples to show that anyone can add a little spark to the everyday, and it doesn't have to be complicated or time-consuming. As a solo founder, I always try to find ways to add memorable moments to the calendar. Last year I started something called 'Booze and Brainstorm', where a friend and I would come together over a couple of cocktails to bounce ideas off each other, just to break the script of being in my own head all the time and to stop everything feeling so serious. I also cross-mentor people in my network, and so every other week we will catch up, offload and be there for one another (side note: mentoring can be really great way for you to appreciate your work more and boost your self-esteem). And for clients and teams I work with now, one of my go-to suggestions is a 'Friday Wins' session. Everyone gets a moment to share something they're proud of, big or small. It's a great way to encourage self-promotion in a safe space and it leaves you ending the week on a high. Not all of these will be your vibe or feel like the right fit, but I would love you to imagine what your week could look like if it had a few more unexpected moments.

How can you shift frustration into celebration? Or boredom into a fun non-negotiable? Here are some questions to ponder on:

- What things do you dread going to and what would make it better?
- What is something memorable you've experienced recently? What can you take away from it or how could you apply it to your own life?
- What things do you hear other companies or workplaces carry out that you wish you did more of in your set-up?

Romanticise your routine

Over the last couple of years, you might have seen a viral lifestyle trend to 'romanticise your life' dominating your social feeds. If you're unfamiliar with the term, life design strategist Georgie Shears explains: 'Romanticising your life is all about finding joy, hidden beauty, magic, significance and meaning in the day-to-day, and the purpose is to enhance your whole experience of life. It's hugely beneficial for better mental health, creativity, increased happiness and fulfilment.'[9] Now before your cynical brain writes this off, I would love you to humour me as we go through some ways you could romanticise your days:

1. **Make your morning routine worth getting up for.** Make a list of things that could help you start your day in the best way or add some extra elements to your existing routine. This could be anything from dancing to your favourite music, making a delicious breakfast or reading ten pages of a book.
2. **Reframe your commute.** Try to make your commute more special by connecting with friends and family, listening to

inspiring content, exploring hobbies, learning something new or just resting (if that's what's most needed!).
3. **Avoid meeting fatigue**. Go through your list of meetings and think about ways you could mix up the format, change the energy or even where you take the calls – walking meetings are a winner, and I've even found standing meetings to be really helpful for reducing the length of them.
4. **Work-station revamp**. What things can you add or remove that will make you feel excited to do your work? It might sound minor but having your favourite stationery, plants, pictures or whatever it is that perks you up nearby can drastically improve how you think about work.
5. **Acknowledge yourself out loud**. Notice the way you talk to yourself and make space to celebrate the things you do. Thank yourself for taking time to meditate and calm your mind, for speaking up and expressing your thoughts clearly and for organising your space to create a peaceful environment.
6. **Say something positive**. Let someone know you're thinking of them, you're proud of their work, or you're grateful of their support. As social creatures, we are wired to form bonds, so saying nice things reinforces these connections and can trigger feelings of warmth and belonging.
7. **Look out for the small sparks**. Instead of searching for fireworks in your day, take note of the small sparks that light you up. Journal them, celebrate them and don't let them slip through.
8. **Make a mood-boosting playlist**. Create a playlist with all your favourite songs to help you through the inevitable highs and lows of work.

9. **Move your body.** Find ways to move your body that don't feel like a chore. Use it to boost your energy and be grateful that you can.

I know these might seem a bit basic or even obvious, but sometimes when we're so far in the depths of feeling like everything is rubbish, it can be easy to overlook the small things that make up our days.

Reframe progression

For so long we've been told that progression is only about looking upwards, that more equals better and that we gain status from reaching higher levels. But when the options to move forward feel stunted, limited or just unavailable, finding ways to cope is essential if you want to stick things out. There's a few sayings and quotes that have helped me personally through these periods that I hope will help you too:

'**Not every season is for blooming**' – Just like in nature, not every part of life is about showing big, visible growth. Some seasons are meant for planting seeds, resting, learning or quietly building. And maybe that's where you are right now, taking notes, soaking things in, and investing in yourself. That's not wasted time; it's how you become stronger, more grounded, and even more of an asset.

'**Celebrate the things that didn't happen**' – In the TED talk, *The Future Will Be Shaped by Optimists*, Kevin Kelly reminded his audience that most of what progress is about is all the things that don't happen. The wars that didn't start, the people that didn't get ill, the animals that didn't go extinct. In a world obsessed with upward progression, this message helps us to see that more doesn't always equate to better, and we can actually be grateful for the things that didn't happen, too.[10]

'Job titles come and go, but they are rented. You don't own them. They will always fall away. What remains true is the story you tell about yourself'[11] – This quote from Thasunda Brown Duckett is such a powerful reminder that the things we often chase, like titles or recognition, aren't permanent. And when we remember that we can't control what we don't truly own, it gets a little easier to let go of the pressure to measure ourselves by things that don't last.

In moments where progression feels stagnant, I recommend that you take these quotes on board and actively find ways to reframe how you define progress. Start measuring growth by who you are becoming, not just what you're being handed. Maybe you're becoming the go-to person for something, maybe you're working more effectively with people, or maybe you're finding ways to have a better work-life balance. Finding small wins, however they might look, is important – plus it's all great evidence to add to your 'Proud Moments' archive that we discussed earlier in this chapter.

When we ask ourselves questions like, 'Why hasn't [insert goal] happened yet?' we can unintentionally stir up fear, doubt and insecurity. Instead of heading down that spiral, try shifting your focus. In a great Harvard Business Review article called *How to Stop Taking Work So Personally*, executive coach and author Melody Wilding suggests a powerful mindset shift to de-identify from your feelings.[12] Try saying things like, 'I'm noticing this feeling, but I'm not this feeling', or 'This thought doesn't have to take over.' It creates just enough space between what you're experiencing and how you respond, meaning you can act with more clarity and less emotional weight. And as you read this, please know a lack of progression is extremely common, especially during economic uncertainty. This situation is not *only* happening to you. Be kind to yourself and remember progress doesn't always look like big wins, it can be quieter and just as meaningful.

* Side note: With all this said, you do deserve to feel valued in your career and if real growth opportunities are opening up somewhere else and your current company can't offer what you need, don't shrink yourself to fit. Always see what's available so you never feel like you've wasted time.

Take control of your own development

As someone who partners with businesses to deliver corporate training and workshops, I've sat in many conversations with HR leaders over the past couple of years who have voiced that they want their *employees* to take the lead on their own progression. This might seem a bit counterintuitive or not how you've done things in the past, but if career development plans aren't being served to you, that shouldn't stop you from being able to grow.

At the time of writing this book, we are seeing companies, particularly in the tech industry, reduce or eliminate DEI (diversity, equity and inclusion) programmes, including learning and development initiatives, due to economic pressures and shifting priorities. For the record, I strongly disagree with this decision – having worked closely with ERGs (Employee Resouce Groups) over the past eight years, it's saddening to see this regression.

I know it's unfair that some companies are pulling back from prioritising development budgets, but I don't want your progression to stand still as a result. Instead of letting the feeling of abandonment consume you, let's flip the script and think instead about how you need to develop to help you achieve your goals. This entire book is about taking back control in your career and, if the right people aren't going to support you to develop, it's time to support yourself.

The plus side of being left to your own devices is that you call the shots and aren't forced to do things you don't want to do.

> Want a mentor to help you grow? = Who can you proactively reach out to within the company or outside of it so that your needs are met?

> Want to upskill and develop in an area? = What skills are going to set you up for your next career success?

And if you're worried about not having that depth of training you deserve, I want to share a piece of advice I heard from Michael Berhane, CEO of POC In Tech. In a video on Instagram he explained that when you're skill stacking, you don't have to be perfect at every individual skill – it's actually okay to be average at some of them. See it like this: if you can add more skills to your CV you start to become so unique people will struggle to compete with you. I'm sure that might be difficult for the perfectionists to stomach, but I include this as a reminder that being 'good enough' at multiple things can help you stand out in this market. So, I want you to experiment, trial things and get used to showing up for yourself, because not every environment you work in will provide you with the right resources you need in order to grow.

TOP TIP: *Although there might be cuts to budgets, don't let this be a reason you don't ask for financial support for training programmes, event tickets or online learning. It's all about pitching to the right people who do hold the purse strings. Try make a business case on how much value you can bring to the company once you've got that development.*

Meet people where they are at

Another challenge you might be facing is the struggle for autonomy or feeling like you're constantly battling micromanagers and being left out of key opportunities. Whilst it's totally fair to fantasise about throwing darts at their photo (we've all been there), I'm going to gently suggest a different approach. Instead of pushing back hard, try meeting them where they're at and finding ways to get them on your side. In the book *Trust and Betrayal in the Workplace,* authors Dennis Reina and Michelle Reina argue that trust is the foundation of every successful workplace relationship and directly impacts team collaboration, employee engagement and overall performance. The book identifies three key dimensions of trust: contractual trust (doing what you say you'll do), communication trust (honest, open dialogue) and capabilities trust (believing in each other's abilities). It delves into the subtle ways trust can be broken, not only through dramatic betrayals but also through missed deadlines, poor communication or exclusion from decisions.[13] I'm not saying you haven't already done more than enough to prove yourself, because you probably have. However, sometimes, it's the relationship that's the real blocker. So, how can you shift that dynamic?

> **Use the same language.** It might seem obvious but when it comes to bonding with people, it's important to find common ground in your communication so they feel like you're both working towards the same outcome. If they are deadline driven, link your contributions back to this and ensure you provide clear updates, stick to timelines and manage expectations if things aren't on schedule. Alternatively, if they are reputation driven, it would be better to focus on communicating how the work you're doing will help improve visibility or

unlock new opportunities for them. These are subtle changes, but you'd be surprised how much of a difference this can make.

Pay attention to their small talk. Start taking note of what they talk about personally and professionally. You might not care about what football team they support or how their kids are getting on at nursery, but trust me when I say their walls will start to come down when you show them a little more attention. Go out of your way to document the non-work discussion points they bring up and be proactive in asking them about it. Sometimes that's all people really need. And whilst we both know it is not your job to take on the emotional labour of making someone feel seen, it might be the strategy that will help you navigate this season of your working relationship.

Try tackling something together. Working on mini projects with a micromanaging boss can be a smart way to build trust and ease tension. Smaller tasks can create low-risk opportunities to show your reliability, communication style and ability to deliver without constant oversight. It's a chance to shift their perception – when they see that you can follow through consistently, they may feel more comfortable about giving you space. Think of it as building blocks: each small win helps prove your capability and strengthens the relationship, making room for more freedom and mutual respect over time.

Get the small stuff right. You might think coming in five minutes late to a meeting isn't a big deal or that your typos in your emails are minor in the grand scheme of things, but irritatingly these things can provide them with ammunition to not trust you. Have a think about some of the areas you might have let lightly slip and make a conscious effort to tweak the habit. I know we're all only human and these things shouldn't define us, but as we move through uncertain times, I just want to make sure that you're not being unfairly punished or discounted from opportunities because of things that are within your reach to change.

Attracting work that aligns with you

The advice that has always stuck with me since my advertising days is: if you want to be known for something you need to show people, not just tell them. I have so many peers who tell me they want to write a book, but then never share their writing publicly or spend time developing their ideas. I know people in my network who say they'd like to build a community but hate speaking to strangers and don't go to events to meet people. As humans we are great at saying what we want to be known for but so often terrible at acting the way we want to be seen. And for clarity, I used to be one of these people.

Six years into my career working in advertising, the cracks of the industry were becoming ever more prominent, and my daily responsibilities were becoming less and less appealing. For as long as I could remember I would often say my biggest ambition was to speak on the TED conference stage one day. But as I sat in a silent office, pushing emails, counting the minutes on the clock go by, I realised I was doing nothing to make TED ever pick up the phone and invite me to speak. I wasn't researching new topics and building a niche or shifting mindsets or challenging the status quo. It was at this point I asked myself: If I were to be invited to speak on the TED stage one day, what would I be speaking about? I loved public speaking, was skilled in marketing and wanted to help people grow. That reflection led to the creation of F*ck Being

CAREER COMEDOWN

Humble, a platform focused on self-promotion, storytelling and challenging the way we show up in our careers. After two and half years of consistency, putting my ideas out in the world and advocating for myself, I was invited to give a TEDx talk.

Not only had I reached a career milestone, but I'd also reshaped my full-time job to align with my passions. Hosting F*ck Being Humble events in my spare time helped me build a reputation at work as an event co-ordinator. It all started when I pitched an idea for Mental Health Awareness Week. My boss said, 'Go ahead, but no help, no budget, and don't let it affect your workload.' Challenge accepted. After late nights, I pulled off an art exhibition in our office basement. It sparked conversations, created a buzz around the office, and proved my value beyond my job title. Soon after, our company began hosting events, and I was asked to help lead them. Event management wasn't part of my role, but my energy made it a no-brainer. We launched a series so successful it toured Amsterdam, New York and the Cannes Lions festival. I was still doing my full-time job, but what fulfilled me was integrating what I loved. That moment taught me the power of shaping your own path. I share this to remind you, what you put out is what you become known for.

But it's not just my story I wanted to share. I spoke to Claire, an animator and director who'd spent twelve years building her reputation. Known for animation, she always aimed to tell more human-led stories. Just as she was preparing to shift into live action, Covid hit and real-world production stalled. Animation demand surged, and Claire found herself in high demand. Whilst grateful at first, it quickly became the only work she was offered, animation was all people associated her with. She ended up feeling stuck, with long days at a screen, difficult clients, little appreciation and poor pay. When we unpacked it, Claire admitted she only self-promoted during quiet periods and mostly accepted whatever came her way.

She had no clear strategy to reposition herself. Towards the end of our conversation, I challenged her to define her non-negotiables, build a promotion plan and rethink how she presented herself. Within minutes, she was buzzing with ideas; it was like a cloud had lifted and she'd stepped out of the trenches.

Both these stories remind us why intentional action is important. It can be so easy for our ambitions to be buried by workloads and doubt, but it's up to you to steer yourself in the right direction. If we want to achieve certain things, we have to be mindful of what we accept and what we're doing to actively attract.

With this in mind, I want you to think about your own situation:

- What would you like to do more of in your career right now?
- How do your actions marry up to your ambitions?
- What content do you need to share that will help you to attract the opportunities you want right now?

Be the change you want to see

In every company you work with or for, there are likely going to be business decisions you don't always agree with. But when you start to feel a significant misalignment, it can feel difficult to stay motivated, especially when the solutions feel obvious to you and others. Whether it's a lack of inclusive policies, bad leadership or a culture that doesn't sit right with you, I want you to remember that you don't have to be in the C-suite to make a difference. Even without a fancy title, your voice and actions can spark change, or at the very least plant the seed for it. I totally get that it might feel disheartening, like nothing you say will matter. But wearing the 'what's the point?' mindset every day only makes it harder to show up.

If your workplace is stuck in its ways or allergic to feedback, just remember that some of the benefits and progress you currently get to enjoy were once someone else's uphill battle. You have the same potential to move the dial, even just a little, for the people who come next. Transformation is hard enough for individuals to achieve, let alone for companies, so you should expect to be met with some resistance. However, here are five steps that will help you start creating change:

1. **Connect with visionaries.** When you're trying to drive change at work, finding visionaries, or people who can see beyond the status quo, is incredibly valuable, even if they're outside your company. Visionaries help you think bigger, see blind spots, and stay inspired when things feel slow or stuck. They've often walked a similar path and can offer the perspective, ideas and encouragement that you won't always find internally. Sometimes, the energy and validation you need to keep going come from someone who's not bound by your company's politics or limitations. Surrounding yourself with bold thinkers helps you stay anchored in possibility and reminds you why change is worth chasing.

2. **Find your internal advocates.** Finding internal advocates starts with noticing who's already speaking up, even in small ways. Look for the people who ask thoughtful questions in meetings, support others' ideas or challenge the status quo with curiosity, not confrontation. They're often the ones quietly influencing culture without needing a spotlight. Start a conversation, share what you've noticed and what you're hoping to change, and see if your goals align. You don't need a big plan, just a shared sense of

what could be better. When you find someone who cares about the same things, you gain not just support but momentum. Change feels lighter together.

3. **Start small to build trust.** When you're trying to make change within a company, aiming for small wins early on is key. Big shifts can feel overwhelming or threatening, especially in workplaces that are resistant to change. They help you build credibility, earn trust and show others that progress doesn't have to be disruptive, it can be thoughtful and steady. Whether it's improving a single process, starting a new conversation or getting one person on board – aim for the micro-yes's and that will lead to the big ones.

4. **Share the progress.** Sharing updates builds visibility and shows others that improvement is happening, even in subtle ways. When people see progress, they're more likely to believe that change is possible and worth investing in. It also invites collaboration, feedback and support, turning your efforts into a shared mission rather than a solo pursuit. Over time, those small moments create a ripple effect, building trust, shifting mindsets and laying the foundation for larger transformations.

5. **Take it external.** Sometimes we are in work environments that condemn our proactivity, and this can feel difficult to sit with. If you're met with significant pushback, my advice to you is to make it your out-of-work project. Your ambition to change something shouldn't be stunted just because you can't make it happen on company time. I'm forever in awe of the community initiatives and grassroots movements that I see popping up in person and online,

and I know all it takes is one person (like you) to have the courage to get the ball rolling. Plus, if you're moving the needle externally and seeing positive results, I would not be surprised if the companies or clients you work with want to jump on the bandwagon.

My hope as you've read through this section is that you can see that change, even if it's incremental, is possible. That you can break the script, romanticise your routine and add more excitement to your days (without having to get it signed off by a CEO). And that no matter what level, age or position you're in, you have the ability to shape a better future for yourself and for others that follow.

Setting Boundaries To Reflect What You Want

I am convinced that setting boundaries effectively could be the answer to all of our problems but the reason we don't do it is that we're still caught in the 'You say jump, I say how high' mindset – a learned behaviour from early childhood experiences which makes it hard to break free from patterns of compliance and self-sacrifice. In a 2022 poll from YouGov, 52 per cent of Americans said they struggle with setting boundaries and saying no when someone asks them for something in the workplace.[14] And in the UK, Headspace's 2025 *Workforce State of Mind* report found that overtime was becoming the norm, with 71 per cent of employees regularly working outside of their scheduled hours weekly.[15]

Please let me state here that I know we don't always have the power to set boundaries. Especially in times of global uncertainty, it's hard to escape the feeling that we should just be grateful for whatever we can get – and yes, in some cases, we might have to bend ourselves more than we'd like. But this shouldn't be representative of our entire work experience. Having no boundaries at all can turn a perfectly enjoyable career into a hellish daily reality, and that is what we want to avoid for you.

So, let's address the elephant in the room in relation to this: professional people pleasing. This is the act of making decisions that will impress other people but ends up making you severely unhappy in the long run. Sound familiar? I thought you might twinge at that. Professional people pleasing is something that can affect high achievers in particular, as you spend so much time prioritising other people's needs without considering what will make you happy. The damaging side effects of this are sustained unfulfilment, exhaustion, overwhelm and burnout, as we push our minds and bodies to the limit. So how do you show your commitment without work taking over your life? Let me talk you through some practical steps.

Ask better interview questions

If you're sticking in your industry, but deciding to change jobs, I want you to make sure that you don't walk into the same disaster zone again. When you move jobs, this is the prime opportunity for you to set the tone or at least have a better chance of influencing how you want to work. But something I see time and time again is that people seem to forget that you are interviewing the company as much as they are interviewing you. I'm not saying you've got all the power, but I wish more people saw interviews as a two-way street. You've got to assess how well the company fits your needs, just as much as they're figuring out if you're the right fit for them. When we don't come in with prepared questions that match what we're looking for, we end up in work environments that are nothing like the shiny, perfect job they sold us, or worse, nothing like what we actually wanted in the first place.

If you've ever been mis-sold a dream role, I'm talking to *you*. I want you to take a minute and jot down all the problems from your previous roles, then turn each of those into a question. Ask yourself: 'Does this new company or client have the same red flags?' I know it sounds obvious, but I cannot tell you how many times I have watched people end up in the exact same toxic situations because they didn't do their homework on the company first. And I promise you can ask these questions without sounding like an interrogator or seeming 'difficult'. Here are some examples:

Previous problem: Bad management
1. How do you measure individual success?
2. How would you describe your ideal employee?
3. How would your direct reports describe your management style?

Previous work problem: Overworked / unsupported:
1. Can you describe a typical workday for someone in this role? Does it typically involve after-hours or weekend work?
2. How does the company handle workload during busy periods?
3. What resources does the company offer to support employee well-being?

Previous work problem: Communication
1. How would you describe the communication style within the team and the company as a whole?
2. How are company decisions made? As an employee is there an opportunity to contribute to company changes?
3. How are disagreements handled within the team?

Previous work problem: Professional growth

1. Can you tell me about the most successful person you ever hired and what they did to be successful?
2. What are people who've been in this role in the past doing now? Where have their careers taken them within this company?

I hope you can see by these examples that there are ways to articulate questions in an interview that will help you to identify whether the role you're applying for is yet another dead end, or if it's more in line with the work you're looking for.

Trusting your gut feeling

I have a friend who is forever saying, 'I just had a bad gut feeling about them.' She can often read people before they've done anything to disappoint her and, even though I often think, 'How could you possibly know that something was off?', 99 per cent of the time she ends up being right.

As I've developed throughout my career, I've come to realise that your gut feeling is often influenced by the experiences you've previously had and is definitely worth listening to. Spotting red flags in people, companies and clients becomes a lot easier when you've weathered storms before; the clues that they are the wrong fit become glaringly obvious. If you get a gut feeling that something's off and you've been stung by that same worry before, do not ignore it. I've taken jobs where I just *knew* I didn't click with the team in the interview, and then had to spend months working with people I'd never vibe with. I've said yes to opportunities with flaky, terrible communicators, and guess what? They stayed flaky and terrible when it came to negotiating and giving feedback. It can take time to develop this sense, but once you do, it's important to factor it properly into your decision-making. One thing I highly recommend doing is creating scoring criteria for evaluating companies, clients or opportunities. Rate them honestly based on your non-negotiables, current needs and your gut feeling. When we're desperate for work, we can end up taking opportunities that we know aren't the right fit, but all that does is delay us from finding what actually works for us.

Love languages at work

A few weeks ago, I jokingly told a friend that I was thinking of sending my client my 'preferred love language', which, for me, is definitely words of affirmation. She laughed and said hers was gifts, so she might just invoice her client for an expensive handbag next time they put her through some drama. As we laughed about what our love languages said about us, it got me thinking that we talk a lot about love languages in our personal lives, but we rarely stop to reflect on or communicate our career love languages. Instead, we make excuses for bosses who will only comment on our work when we've done something wrong, never when we've done something right. Or we accept barely being rewarded because we've fallen into the trap of working at a company that considers everyone part of the 'family'.

Gary Chapman and Paul White took the concept of love languages and applied it to the workplace in their book *The 5 Languages of Appreciation in the Workplace*.[16] I wanted to share some of them with you in a work context to see which you might prioritise in your career:

> **Words of Affirmation.** You are someone who appreciates genuine positive feedback. The occasional 'Good work!' won't suffice; you want people to recognise the lengths you've gone to and acknowledge it with a heartfelt recognition of how you've gone above and beyond.

Quality Time. You are someone who wants the other person to listen and allow you to express your ideas at length, you want people to give you undivided attention. These people make themselves available to guide you but also create space for you to shine.

Acts of Service. You are someone who values people who do things not just say things. When you're swamped, you want your colleague or boss to see that and offer to support. When they offer to alleviate that work, it shows you they recognise how much you do and how much they value you.

Giving Tangible Gifts. It's not about the cost of the gift or materialistic prizes, but small tokens or gestures that show the person bought you something you might appreciate.

As you read through the list of professional languages of appreciation, I want you to honestly reflect on how regularly, if ever, you've vocalised these preferences to people at work. I imagine a lot of you will be thinking never, or definitely not enough. And this is why I want you to be thinking more intentionally about how you can communicate your preferences in order to make sticking in the industry more enjoyable. People are not mind readers and when it comes to appreciation languages, most people are way more likely to give you what they would want to receive, rather than what you actually need.

If you're truly wanting to 'stick' in your career and change the way you work with others, figuring this out will strengthen your work relationships and help to prevent future misunderstandings and frustrations. Plus, knowing the career appreciation language of those around you means you can adjust your behaviour to create a more balanced, supportive dynamic too. I know the thought of opening up this conversation might feel a bit awkward at first, but referencing this book is a way in . . . 'I'm reading this book called *Career Comedown,* and one of the things it mentions is applying appreciation languages to work relationships. Have we ever tried this as a company?' And when they inevitably say, 'No', that's your golden opportunity to explain your own appreciation language and introduce the idea.

Of course, I caveat all of these recommendations by saying I cannot control how people respond to you communicating your preferences. However, this whole chapter is about doing things that might make you feel uncomfortable but will hopefully get you better results.

So, let's think about how you could communicate your languages in real-time situations to better improve your relationships with others:

Dialogue with manager

I'm really keen to get the most out of our working relationship and communicate with you as effectively as possible, so I thought it would be useful if we both discussed our preferences on communication in relation to:

Feedback – how do we prefer to receive feedback?

Conflict – how do we prefer to handle a problem?

Progress – how do we motivate one another?

Successes – how do we show appreciation for each other?

I understand that not everyone has the same approach, but I'd really like to do my best to support you as well as I can and vice versa.

Ways of working document

If you are working for yourself and you want to find a better work-life balance, you need to realise you are your own boss and you can set the tone of your working relationships. Far too often I watch self-employed workers become slaves to their clients and work themselves into the ground, all because they didn't set their preferences upfront. One of the best things about being self-employed is that you have more control over the way you work, so if you've not done so already, set up a 'Ways of Working' document that is shared with all clients as an onboarding process. Don't worry, I don't mean owning up to the fact you have Netflix on in the background, you start Happy Hours at 4pm on a Friday or that you take three-hour leisurely lunches during the middle of the day. Those things can be your own secrets to keep. I mean spelling out how you plan to work, without it being dictated by your client first.

I first received a document like this when I booked time with a virtual assistant to help me with admin-related tasks. After agreeing fees and availability, Alanah shared her 'Ways of Working' document, which included things like working hours, communication style and feedback rounds. What I thought was particularly smart about this approach was that I (the client) had to sign the agreement before the work commenced. It was written in a formal yet approachable tone of voice, and it was a common practice that Alanah had integrated into her process in order to ensure her time and energy were protected. As a self-employed business owner, my immediate reaction was 'How smart – I wish I'd have thought of this for myself.' I was so used to operating in a 'customer is always right' mentality, that I hadn't even considered the power I had to shape my working relationships. You might be reading this thinking, 'There's no way I could get my clients to sign something like this.' I understand.

I've had clients who can't even pay their invoices on time, let alone sign off on agreeing to my preferred ways of working. But at least *write* this document out. You don't have to ask them to sign anything (unless they're actually reliable, then go for it), but you can absolutely bring it up in your initial meetings to set the tone for how you want the relationship to go. I've said it once, and I'll say it again: you didn't quit your job to have zero boundaries and get treated worse than you did when you were a full-time employee. So, if you have even the slightest chance of influencing how you work with someone, don't you think it's worth a shot? You might be surprised by how setting expectations upfront can save you a lot of headaches later on.

Get comfortable with the uncomfortable

When you're working for a company as an employee, a lack of boundaries is basically a ticking time bomb. It leads to either a bunch of unhappy, unproductive employees, or worse, employees quitting, leaving a skills gap that the company has to scramble to fill. Neither of these are a win for the company. So, stop worrying that setting boundaries is going to wreck your reputation. What actually looks bad is you being miserable, slacking off or becoming that person who's hard to work with because you didn't speak up about what you need. Instead, I want you to see setting boundaries as something you are doing to help your company get the best from you. You're not asking for too much, you're not being demanding and you're definitely not disengaging just because you've decided to voice your preferences. The reason so many of us work in boundaryless chaos is because we're scared of having those uncomfortable conversations. But I need you to remember that sixty minutes of an awkward meeting is worth it if you get to find a lifetime of work happiness because you voiced what you wanted.

Below are a few examples of how you can communicate your preferences with regards to setting boundaries with your work colleagues.

Contact out of hours
The lines between work and personal life really started to blur once we all began working from home during the pandemic. Whether it was intentional or not, many of us found ourselves working beyond our usual hours, and before we knew it, it became the new normal. For some, it's been tough to break out of that pattern. It's especially tricky when colleagues are continuing conversations past working hours. If this sounds familiar, it's time to reset some boundaries and establish clearer expectations.

You can do this by using phrases like:

If your colleagues contact you out of hours
- 'Unless the situation is urgent, I'll reply to any communications I get after I've left the office the following day. Can we confirm together what we deem to be urgent?'
- 'I know you often catch up on your emails out of hours, but when I see the emails pop up late at night, I feel a sense of expectation to reply. Would you be open to scheduling your emails so they arrive in my inbox the next morning?'
- 'I know other people in the office use WhatsApp to send updates, but I'd prefer for all of our communications to be done via email – please can you schedule any future messages this way.'

If your boss piles it on and on and on
- 'I'm currently at my max capacity, in order for me to take on additional work I'll need to re-prioritise my

workload. Can you please advise on what you would like me to focus my energy on right now?'
- 'I'm really happy that you feel you can trust me with this responsibility, but in order for me to do my best job, I will need extra support from another team member to help with my existing workload.'
- 'Since starting in the role, my responsibilities have expanded beyond my current job specification, and I'd like to talk to you about how we can rebalance my workload as I'm currently feeling overstretched.'

If you need to say no after already committing
- 'When I offered to get involved in the project, I thought I had more capacity than I do. However, I'm struggling to juggle both sets of responsibilities and I don't want any mistakes to be made as a result.'
- 'Although I'd love to continue supporting on this, I currently have tasks with a more time-sensitive deadline, so moving forward I will only be able to allocate xxxx.'
- 'Based on my current schedule, I'm not going to be able to allocate enough time to this. I have spoken to [insert colleague's name] and they would love to gain more experience and can offer a hand instead.'

If people distract you / don't give you space
- 'Thanks for the update, in the future are you okay to update me via email once a day so I can review the status in my own time?'
- 'I work better when I can have undisturbed time for two to three hours at a time, so can we check in at midday and end of day?'

- 'Don't worry about updating me after. I'll drop you a message when I have time in my diary to hear the result.'

These are just a few examples of situations where you might need to set boundaries, but it's important to make sure you are clearly communicating how you'd like to work with people and explaining why where possible. If the people you are speaking to can understand why you would prefer to work in this way, they are more likely to adhere to and respect your wishes.

For any boomers or millennials reading this, I urge you to take inspiration from Gen-Z's creative writing skills. You only have to type into Google 'Best Gen-Z Out of Office emails' and you're met with a list of hilarious tradition-breaking responses. Here's a couple that might make you smile:

Subject: *Out of Office – Pretending I'm on Holiday*

Message:
Hi! I'm out of the office pretending to be on a holiday, but in reality, I'm just staying at home and pretending to get my life together. If this is an emergency, please contact [colleague's name]. Otherwise, I'll get back to you once I've realised it's 5:00 p.m. and I should probably be working. 😊

Subject: *Out of Office – Watching My Favourite Series*

CAREER COMEDOWN

> *Message:*
> Hi there! I'm currently out of the office, binge-watching my favourite Netflix series (please don't judge me). I'll be back after finishing Season 6, Episode 3, which is expected to take me until [date]. If it's urgent, I'll pause the show and get back to you. Otherwise, enjoy your day, and may you find peace in your own binge-watching journey. 🍿 📺
>
> *Subject:* Out of Office – Mood Is Too Much
> *Message:*
> I'm out of the office, probably in my feelings, listening to sad music, or contemplating life's biggest questions like 'What is the meaning of email?' I'll be back when I've sorted out my emotions. If it's urgent, try [colleague's name] – they're probably less dramatic than I am. 🥀

Depending on what industry you're in, these might not get the desired response you're looking for, but it's just a reminder that you don't have to take setting boundaries so seriously. Like it or loathe it, the younger generations are doing a much better job of articulating their preferences without panicking they'll lose their job as a result. Something we could all do with bearing in mind!

Career-Moulding Conversations

Throughout this book we've been reflecting on all the things that you enjoy, all the things that are lacking, and all the ways you can make solo change. But now I want to help you with tackling the conversation of change with others. If you want to mould your career into something you look forward to and feel proud of, let's go through exactly how you can negotiate your preferences:

Step 1: Get clear on the company goals

One of the biggest mistakes I see people continuously make in their career is not having a clear understanding of what the company's objectives are. I'm not talking about your job title or your daily responsibilities; I'm talking about what the business is working towards. Every year the company you work for will map out targets and metrics that they will use to measure the success of the company's performance – whether that's successfully entering new markets, growing higher profit, improving client retention, attracting more customers or reducing the overall company costs. Every single person at the company needs to know what the business objectives are so that they can link their performance back to the metrics and be fairly reimbursed for their contribution.

TOP TIP: *Career comedown or not, I need you to set up meetings with your bosses or line managers and ask them, 'How are we measuring the success of the company this year and for the next five years?' This question will help you to track how your time is best spent, and it will enable you to gather the most relevant examples of how you're working towards the company goals. Beyond being celebrated for your performance, asking this question is particularly important for anybody who wants to mould their careers. If you don't know what the company's ambitions are, your request to mould your responsibilities in a certain direction could easily be rejected if it doesn't marry up with the business plans. If you want to build a successful case for you to do more or less of something, you have to show how it will benefit the company.*

CAREER COMEDOWN

> **Example:**
>
> **Reason for your career comedown:** You've lost the spark in your work because everything you pitch gets rejected and so your days have become really formulaic.
>
> **Where you're going wrong:** You're letting 'no's get in the way of you pitching ideas that you're excited about.
>
> **What you could do to change this:** Get clearer on why the answer is no and figure out what will get a yes. What is getting approved, and how can you align your ideas to what they are looking for? Even if that means doing less exciting work to start, this could build trust and the permission to do more exciting things in the future.

And if you're self-employed, the same applies to you. Beyond the tasks you are contracted to do, you need to be asking bigger, more strategic questions that will help you in the future. Instead of just being briefed by a client, you should be proactively asking about their overall business plans outside of what you've been tasked to explore to ensure you can upsell and re-pitch yourself for continuous work.

> **Example:**
>
> **Reason for your career comedown:** You want to be earning significantly more money, but you feel capped at your day rate, and don't know how to secure bigger budgets.

> **Where you're going wrong:** You receive a brief, but you only ask questions about the project timings, deliverables and requirements.
>
> **What you could do to change this:** Make a list of questions that could help you with pitching in a higher-priced product. These might include:
>
> - Outside of this brief, what are your ambitions for this year?
> - Do you work with other suppliers? If so, are you happy with their delivery?
> - Are there any other areas that you're struggling to crack?
> - How do you allocate your budget for suppliers, is there a key metric you measure?
> - What has been your biggest investment in the company yet?

These are just a few examples of how questions about the overall client's process and ambitions could help you to build a product that they need, and that they are willing to spend more money on. If you want to be seen as a supplier worth investing higher budgets in, you need to be asking the right questions, that will help to inform your pitch. In Zoe Chance's book *Influence is your superpower* she shares a magic question that consists of four key words, 'What would it take?' as a tool for influencing outcomes. This question can be used for negotiating salaries, 'What would it take for me to be considered for the next salary bracket?' or could be used for collaboration, 'What would it take for you to choose this option and feel confident in it?'. What makes this question so powerful is that it shifts you away from disappointment and moves you toward clarity and possibility.

In both instances, the more you know about what motivates the decision-makers (and the people who control the money), the better you will be able to pitch your preferences or yourself back to them.

Step 2: Get your case studies ready

People don't respond that well to change, especially if it's something they've not experienced before. So, whether it's internal or external, I want you to find examples of how other businesses are flexing to adapt to employees' needs and how your company could do the same. A great example of this is Shopify's recent move to create 'dual tracks', giving employees two career progression ladders to choose from – one for people who want to be managers and the other for individual contributors who don't see being a manager as part of their journey. The decision to do this stemmed from the company identifying that their most creative contributors stopped being creative because they were overburdened with managing people – a role many of them didn't want in the first place. The company decided to create two paths that give individuals the autonomy to choose how they progress. This solution helps to retain talent, boost productivity and attract fresh new talent by using an alternative progression plan. When you are trying to pitch something that a company hasn't done before, the more ammunition and evidence you have in favour of it, the better.

Here are a couple of other case studies you might find handy and useful, depending on what aspect of your career you're trying to mould:

- Google encourages employees to explore new roles and projects through its '20% time' policy, where employees can dedicate a portion of their workweek to projects outside their immediate responsibilities. This approach has fostered a culture of innovation, employee growth and cross-functional collaboration.
- TOMS shoes started The Tomorrows Project. Each month, employees can submit a forward-thinking idea that supports organisations they are inspired by; the only requirements are that it has to benefit others and be able to get off the ground within ninety days. Each peer-chosen project is given financial and administrative support from TOMS to help make the biggest impact.
- Smith Hospital has created a nursing job rotation programme that allows nurses to work in new departments rotationally. Smith Hospital rotates nurse assignments every quarter across departments such as the emergency room, psychiatric wards, intensive care and surgery recovery. This allows the nurses to have a greater understanding of how every department in the hospital works and also reduces burnout in the nurses, as the stress of each department varies, and the change prevents anyone getting too overloaded.

I share these examples as they are all unique ways companies created systems and initiatives that helped retain talent and keep them feeling engaged. A very simple activity you can do is google 'best employee engagement case studies' and see what examples jump out at you. Sometimes we don't always know what we want when we're having a career comedown, so I recommend seeking out inspiration from businesses that are leading the way to see what reignites that spark.

Step 3: Do the working out so they don't have to

Have you ever said no to something before you properly reviewed the idea because it sounded more hassle than it's worth? That's generally why a lot of new suggestions in the workplace get rejected. If it feels too costly, time-intensive or unlikely to have a quick return on investment, people will shut down an idea to make it go away, so you need to make your request as easy as possible for someone to say yes to. Instead of solely pitching an adjustment to your working approach, you should explicitly map out the steps that need to be taken for it to become a reality – ideally, those steps should be so simple that it feels immediately attainable.

In his book *Never Split the Difference*, which teaches you how to negotiate like an FBI hostage handler, author Chris Voss shares a technique called the accusation audit.[17] This is a pre-emptive negotiation technique where you list and address the worst accusations your counterpart could make against you. This approach can defuse potential defences and establish a groundwork for productive dialogue. For example, charity fundraisers are often met with rejection when they are asking for donations on the streets. Common initial responses they may get are: 'I don't have money on me', 'I'm in a rush' or 'I don't donate to charities.' However, you'll often find that before you've even opened your mouth, they will beat you to it by saying:

- 'Don't worry if you're not carrying cash, I can take a card payment today.'

- 'I can see you're in a rush, but this will take less than two minutes of your time.'
- 'Would you be able to live comfortably with £15 less in your account?'

They know that if they can acknowledge the reasons for your resistance before you do, you will have less of an excuse to say no.

Now, I can't guarantee that the company or clients you work with will say yes to every request because the sad reality is they are looking out for themselves more than they are looking out for you. But remember, a negative response in a negotiation isn't always a bad thing. In fact, if you read ANY sales negotiation book, they will remind you that a 'no' doesn't necessarily close the door on the negotiation, it can often open it wider. It forces both sides to clarify their positions, rethink their strategy and can lead to a solution that benefits both sides. It's vital to make sure that you understand why you're getting the 'no' in order to evaluate whether it's something that could be renegotiated again or whether you have to accept it and move elsewhere.

Dialogue checklist:

- Verbalise the accusation before they raise it.
- Communicate the business benefit.
- Recommend a strategy.
- Offer your time to make it happen.
- Re-emphasise why this would help the business.

Step 4: Don't fight the market

When I quit my job to run my side hustle as full-time business in March 2020, I had lined up six months' worth of paid work and a healthy pipeline of projects. Then bam. Three weeks later, the entire country went into lockdown, and work as we knew it was about to change forever. The employee training workshops I'd lined up were instantaneously scrapped because they weren't exactly 'top priority' anymore and my revenue forecast pretty much vanished overnight.

I remember the feeling so clearly: I went from cloud nine that I'd finally plucked up the courage to leave to plummeting back down to earth questioning how I could make it work. At this point I had officially reached my career comedown limit and had vowed I wouldn't go back to the advertising industry. So much so, that when my old company reached out to ask if I needed part-time work whilst I figured things out, I politely and firmly said, 'No thanks!' This was my time, and I was ready to stand on my own two feet.

Instead of sticking to my original plan of chasing corporate clients, I decided to flip the script and focus on actually helping people through the pandemic because that's what the world needed. Was I making as much money as I did in my full-time job? Nope. Was I hitting the numbers I'd predicted for the next six months? Definitely not. But people were desperately seeking out career advice, and I wanted to offer it. Over the next eighteen months, I hosted an online workshop almost every week, grew our audience from 5,000 to 25,000 followers organically (thank you, to my OG followers!), and helped a lot of people who were struggling. And when the dust settled and we started to emerge from the pandemic, the corporate clients suddenly started knocking on my door again.

What I learned from this far from fairytale start to running my business, was the importance of being strategic, flexible and not wallowing over what could've been. Yes, I'd quit my job to work less hours and make more money as a consultant, but sadly that wasn't the card I was dealt at that time. People praised me for how quickly I pivoted to make things work online, but the truth is, I didn't have time to mourn the loss of my original plans. I had to adapt, respond to what the market was throwing at me, and make my skills work in the here and now. I share all of this to say that we all have big career goals, but sometimes the universe has other plans and we don't always get to choose the order in which we achieve them. Fast forward four years and I'm now living out that original dream, speaking internationally, having sold over 10,000 copies of my first book, and now writing my second. It was absolutely a longer journey than I had planned and there were definitely times when I could have thrown in the towel, but rearranging my ambitions was what powered me through.

Although we're more than five years on since the pandemic hit, we're still seeing the impact of uncertain markets reroute our decision-making. Take Kim Darragon, marketing consultant and founder of Kim Does Marketing who works predominantly with small business founders to build marketing strategies. After a two-year stint in LA, she returned to London in 2024 hoping to resume her freelance business as usual only to find that her usual small business clients were not spending what they previously were. Lowering her rates was not an option, so Kim repositioned her offering and pitched herself as a fractional head of marketing, helping mid-sized businesses tackle bigger strategies, while providing leadership for their junior marketing teams. What I love about this example is her reactive approach. Kim didn't spend six months wasting her energy on selling herself to people who couldn't afford her; she looked for the clients that could and pitched her skills to them on her own terms.

Here's the truth: the people who see the best results in their careers aren't the ones who give up when things don't go according to plan. They're the ones who know how to play the hand they're dealt and play it *well*.

Step 5: Make sure everyone is listening

In the workplace many of us want to make our voices heard but we're not thinking about how to create a better environment for listening. On the podcast 'How to be a better human', international speaker and trainer Julian Treasure explains one of his tactics to encourage better listening is setting up agreements or 'listening contracts' before making a request. For example, you might say, 'Hi Chris, do you have five minutes to give me your undivided attention?' If they say no, you can ask when would be a good time and schedule a moment that works for both of you. This way, if they're distracted during your conversation, it's easier to remind them that you were expecting their full attention and that you're not feeling heard. He also explained the importance of not overfilling the conversations you have with too much pre-amble and instead getting to the *why* upfront so you can captivate them immediately. He described a system called 'Say, Say, Say' which is a technique to make sure you engage the person you're speaking to and it's clear what they need to do next.

1. Say what you're going to say – 'I'm speaking to you to today to discus . . .'
2. Say the thing – 'The thing I would like to do is . . .'
3. Say what you said – 'So if this is an option, I would love to do . . .'

But it's not just about framing your own conversations for listening success, you also need to reflect on how and when you are actively listening in your daily interactions too. Recently, I attended an event where business leader Karen Blackett OBE shared a brilliant insight: if you want to see more progress, arrive at meetings twenty minutes early and stay thirty minutes after. Arriving early allows time for small talk that helps you understand what people are juggling and where their focus is. Staying afterwards gives space for what often goes unsaid in the meeting itself. Hearing this made me think of all the times in my career when the most valuable insights didn't come from the boardroom, but from the informal conversations in between, the quick chats and the post-meeting debriefs. So, if you're preparing to pitch to a client or a boss, consider where you can listen more actively beyond the formal decision-making moments.

Let go of what you can't control

So far, I've shared a lot about the proactive steps you can take to shape your career, but – let's be honest – you can't control everything or everyone around you. If you want to thrive, you've got to get smart about managing what's outside of your control.

When I spoke to Liz Ward, a career coach and founder of coaching platform Slick Pivot, about this, she explained that one of the most powerful shifts we can make is in how we choose to think about a situation. For example, let's say you really want to stick in your career, but you've got a boss you are convinced is trying to make your life a living hell. Instead of accepting this as the ultimate truth, Liz challenges you to flip the script, explaining that, 'The way you experience your world reflects your beliefs. Some beliefs help you, while others may make things harder. Take a step back and ask yourself: what belief about this situation would serve me better right now?' Liz is right, holding onto the belief that your boss is out to get you only drains your energy. Would it be way more freeing to walk into the office every day, assuming that deep down they want you to do well, and they are struggling under pressure, too?

Brené Brown, the best-selling author and researcher, also talks about this in an interview with Oprah Winfrey, where she highlights that humans create narratives to make sense of the pain they feel. That narrative doesn't have to be based on facts – our brains crave story, any story, just to ease the discomfort of uncertainty, and suddenly a single dismissive glance from a coworker can instantly become 'I knew she didn't like me.'[18] To help with this and to shield yourself from slight changes in other people's moods, Liz recommends 'empathy mapping' or reflecting from someone else's shoes. You can ask yourself, 'What might they be feeling or experiencing right now?' Exercising compassion helps you detach from taking things too personally and, ultimately, to protect your energy better.

Interview Spotlight

I spoke to Lisa, a creative director, who, despite navigating motherhood and other life changes, has stuck out a career in the creative industry.

Tell me about the start of your career journey?

My career has come in four chapters. Chapter one spans the decade before having children. I began on a high point quickly getting into some high-profile projects soon after graduating – I was working as a freelance assistant animator for advertising, pop promos, and live rock concerts which was exciting and unique work at large scale. So I thought my portfolio would stand out, but over a few years the projects would still dry up and I'd struggle to find creative work. With only myself to look after, I was able to stick to my goals and upskilled myself – the industry was going through a period of digitising, so I realised to stand out I would need new skills and I taught myself After Effects and programming. Doing this got me a fulltime job as a multimedia designer in a large experiential agency and allowed me to remain in the industry.

After these first ten years, you decided to start a family. How did that change your relationship with work?

The second chapter was post-kids. I took nine months maternity leave, but could see my industry, and the work environment (long hours, deadline-driven, in an office) wasn't conducive to having a family so I was very worried about returning to work. I tried a new agency but this was a mistake because the working environment was the same, only now I didn't even know anyone in the company. I felt guilty leaving early everyday to get to the childminder and it often raised eyebrows with the other staff – flexible working was not a thing in 2007 – I only managed three months there before resigning. My career was still important but no longer the priority. As a family we decided to move out of London to Kent and reduce our mortgage, and this gave me time to pivot my career again. I needed to be my own boss so I set up my own branding business and over five years I slowly built a flexible career that suited me and my family. This allowed me to have my second child with minimal upheaval but maintain my design skills which was really important to my sense of self. Chapter three came after another massive life change. My husband died and I was left on my own with two young children in Kent and no family support. That forced my hand again as I had to reconsider what I was doing and how I was going to do it. With my bereavement I came into a small amount of money, enough to start investing in property, so for the first time in my life I left the creative industry to do something completely different. I spent a year studying property management, going to seminars, reading books, joining property groups and re-educating myself. I'd had so much turmoil that doing something completely different was actually really refreshing. Nobody knew who I was, and I didn't have any expectations.

What did stepping out of your career teach you?

It was eyeopening. I made money, lost money, got ripped off and met some unpleasant people. Sometimes you need to work somewhere else, to see how it compares – the grass isn't always greener! I did it for a year, got my various investments sorted out and then went back into the creative industry, freelancing and eventually co-founding a creative studio. I had missed being creative, the identity it gives you! I come back to your purpose. I know my core being is a creative one. So, anything that doesn't fulfil that is never going to satisfy me.

What advice would you give to people who are unhappy in their career, but don't feel ready to leave their situation?

I manage a number of young women now, and I encourage them to be proactive in asking for what they need. Don't be afraid to ask for pay rises or promotions, it will keep you growing, even if you get pushed back. Asking for something is a form of power because it forces an answer from somebody else and gives you some control over your situation and allows you to take action. If you just sit still, nothing will change, so start making small changes yourself. Look at what you're doing and identify what's causing you to be unhappy. Is there a sideways step you can take that won't upend your life? Are you bored? Can you learn new skills and retrain on the job? If you're not learning, then you'll never feel challenged. And never stop networking. My network has proven invaluable over the last twenty-five years and I've found every new role through my network organically. Many creatives find that approach difficult, but you just never know what's going to happen and you must protect yourself - even if you aren't ready to leave your situation, your company could go bust tomorrow, so it's worth being prepared for anything! Rather than seeing it as networking for networking's sake, think of it as making friends and keeping an interest in what people are doing - this might help improve your situation naturally. I'm not a great networker but I'm good enough – you only have to be good enough!

What factors should people consider before leaving a career?

Be careful if you are both leaving your career and changing location, that's a lot of change in one go. I left my career, left London, and had a child all at the same time – not ideal from a career point of view and I had to rebuild my social life as well. Timing is also key – it takes about eighteen months before you reach peak productivity in a new position and truly settle into a new job role – can you accommodate that stress? Have you got the funds to cover you if it doesn't work out in those eighteen months? Can you keep a window open with your old career? So try not to burn any bridges! It depends on your age when changing careers, but now that I'm older I have less time to waste figuring out new filing systems and the politics of a new business. Learning new skills is fun, but I can't afford to make any mistakes with my time, it's too valuable. So if there's a way that you can reskill, retrain or reconfigure your working life within your existing setup, think it through carefully.

How important has setting boundaries been for sticking?

Choice is what is important and my choice is to be quite flexible. I needed flexibility after I had my children, so I had fewer boundaries with clients – I was happy to take calls on a weekend, for example, because I knew that I wouldn't be working during the weekdays between certain hours. Now I'm at an agency again, I set more boundaries and this helps keep my work life balance better than when I was in my twenties when I lived for work. So I don't agree with rigid rules – it's not always possible to switch on and switch off outside of working hours if you're doing something vocational. There's a nice proverb that I like: 'The tree that bends in the wind doesn't break.' I think it's good to have some boundaries, but to keep them a little bit fuzzy.

Stick – Final Thoughts

Throughout this Stick chapter we've explored a range of ways that you can make positive changes in your working life to more closely align your current job/industry with your needs. The most crucial element I want to flag is ***commitment***.

Commitment to:

- Having regular self-check-ins.
- Honest conversations.
- Celebrating what's working / noting down what's not.
- Believing in yourself enough to push for what you want.

If you're going to stick with your career and evolve within it, you've got to be willing to let go of the drama that's led you here and really reflect on how your actions might be contributing to your situation, as well as assessing the external factors. But remember, operating with a 'one-foot-in-one-foot-out' mindset isn't going to cut it, so if you want to avoid going round in circles you have to be open to starting with a clean slate. It's time to break the cycle of excuses, and start self-reflecting, pushing through challenges and getting clearer on the boundaries you need in order to have a happy work life. There was a reason you were drawn to this industry or role in the first place, you just need to reconnect with what that is.

Remember, nothing changes if nothing changes.

CHAPTER 4
TWIST

WHAT TO DO WHEN YOU WANT TO CHANGE LANES

In the game blackjack, you twist when you think there could be a better option available. You're not confident that your hand will win the game, so you're willing to gamble it all to land the right card. If you're choosing to twist in your career right now, you're hoping that there is a better way of working out there for you and you want to take the risk to see how it unfolds. Like blackjack, I can't promise that you'll immediately find that winning card when you choose to twist, but I can assure you that you won't constantly be questioning 'what if'.

This chapter is for anyone who wants to take the leap, mix things up, follow their dreams or discover what their new ambitions are. It's for the people who have come to the realisation that their current path isn't their final destination, and who want to explore where other routes could take them. I knew I was ready to twist when I realised I was persevering down a path that I no longer fantasised about. My optimism for the industry was dying and the more I climbed the ladder, the more I saw its flaws. I got the 'why' behind all the business decisions (that I still didn't agree with), but the fun of my job was being drained by protocols and people I didn't enjoy working with. Early on in my career, I remember my old manager telling me she didn't want to be promoted to director level because it became less rewarding and more political. At the time, I was so fixated on climbing the ladder and earning more I thought her choice bizarre – now I understand exactly what she meant. It was becoming more evident to me that what I really valued from work was variation. I loved being around new people, I wanted more independence, fewer layers of hierarchy, more creativity and, most of all, I wanted to express myself without a million layers of company red tape. I'm so grateful for all the experiences I had during my advertising career, but I knew when I accepted my final job in the industry that I was DONE if it didn't work out. Three months later, I had handed in my notice and pursued my dream of being a public speaker. I haven't looked back since.

Out of the three options, Stick, Twist or Tap Out, I'd say this one carries the most risk. I'm not saying this to scare you but to remind you that this journey is more likely to feel like a rollercoaster of emotions than any other option, because you're trying something completely new. But rather than be fearful of that idea, I can only encourage you to be excited about the unknown.

That was my story, but here's some other reasons why you might be feeling drawn to twist:

The dream chasers

After years of chewing off friends' ears down the pub about the life you could have had, you're finally making the decision to put your money where your mouth is and go after your dream career. Even you have got bored of being all talk and no action, so this is your moment, the thing you've been desperately waiting for all this time. There might have been obstacles along the way, but you know this is the right time for you and you're ready to spread your wings and flourish in a completely new way. You're excited by the future, and you know that betting on yourself is what you will need to do at this point in your career.

Something's gotta give

You might not be chasing a dream, in fact you may have no idea what your dream is, but you do know you've got to get out now, because something has to change. Your decision might be motivated by money, needing flexibility, hating your boss or colleagues, the need to spend more time with family, burnout or just the fed-up feeling of working on something that you no longer care about. Whatever your reason, please don't put pressure on yourself for your next move to have to be THE move. You're making your decision out of necessity, because the way you're functioning isn't sustainable. It's okay if your journey is a little more squiggly and not immediately obvious. Just like dating, you might have to kiss a few frogs before you find exactly what it is that you're looking for – but the longer-term payoff will be better than staying in your current situation.

An unexpected twist

For some of you reading this, the decision to twist might not have actually been initiated by you. You may have been affected by layoffs or redundancies and are now considering reinventing yourself. It's a scary time, but I don't want you to let the fear take full control. Whether you're working a long notice period or have been terminated effective immediately, please know you're not alone. Although it might feel like a total shock to the system and not what you were anticipating, this is an opportunity for you to reflect on what you want to do next. When speaking to the F*ck Being Humble community about this topic, the common feedback I received was to take your time to re-evaluate what you are looking for and be extremely open to what the 'next step' could look like. Not everything has to be a destination; it can be a stepping stone in your career.

Good reasons to twist	Bad reasons to twist
You've exhausted all your options in your current industry	You've had a bad day, week or month. Let's not make this decision too quickly
There's always been something pulling you in this direction and you're over people pleasing	You're being swayed by other people's success stories
You recognise your current industry constraints and the likelihood of them ever changing is slim	You think it will be easier than your current situation
You don't like your current clients, boss or colleagues, so you think twisting is better	You're running away from sitting with your emotions and don't want to register your own contributions to the situation you're in

So now we've explored what might have led you here, I want to share a concept with you that will hopefully stick in your mind as you navigate the highs and lows of this next chapter.

Avoiding boldness regret

#NOREGRETS is meant to be a positive outlook that helps you to stop lingering on things that you didn't do and start focusing on all the things you can do. Whilst I've whispered this to myself after doing something I most definitely would regret, over the last two years my perspective on this topic has been swayed by behavioural psychologist Daniel Pink. In his most recent book, *The Power of Regret*, he debunks the myth of the 'no regrets' philosophy of life and dedicates a large portion of his time asking people in the later years what they most regret not doing in life.[1] Out of the four main types of regrets people have, the one that really hit home for me (and I want it to hit home for you too) is what he calls **Boldness Regret**. Boldness regret is all about the chances we didn't take, the opportunities we didn't grab when we had the chance. It's the moments we didn't act, like when you had that killer idea at work but didn't speak up, or when you passed on that exciting job offer in another city. Many of my followers who are older will say to me, 'God I wish I'd have heard from you sooner in my career, I wouldn't have wasted all that time worrying about what people thought and just gone after what I wanted.' My response to that is, always, that it's never too late. So, before we go any further into this chapter, I want you to pause for a second and reflect on your own boldness regrets. They might just be the signpost for what you don't want to repeat in this next chapter of your life.

- What do you regret not saying yes to?
- What do you regret not chasing after?
- If the opportunity came around again, what would make you feel more open to saying yes?

Now we've reflected on what you already regret not doing, let's start talking about the mindset changes you may need to make in order to ensure you don't repeat these same regrets.

Things To Unlearn

Before I take you through the mindset shifts of how to 'twist', I first want to guide you through a few things you need to unlearn in order to move forward successfully. Before you can open yourself up to new perspectives, I need you to discard some of your outdated ones.

Other people's values overtake my own

Other people's values all need to be deprioritised when you choose to twist. If you're honest with yourself, the external pressures you feel from other people are probably what led you to pick up this book in the first place. If you want to start afresh or turn the page to a new chapter, you need to get really comfortable with what *you* truly value and stop trying to please everyone else. If your parents don't get your decision, let them figure it out in their own time. If your friends think you're crazy for walking away from something stable, let them stay up all night worrying. Remember, you're building the life you want based on *your* desires, not on society's idea of what the 'right' path is. So, it's time to stop asking for permission and start moving towards what *you* really want.

TOP TIP: *Something that I've found particularly useful when communicating my career change (especially to the people who love quizzing me on the title of my first book) is to have a list of responses ready to navigate situations when people inevitably question your motives for switching things up. Let's explore some examples:*

Them: I can't believe you'd leave behind a career that you've spent so many years chasing. Are you sure you want this?!

Your response: I appreciate your concerns, but I've changed as a person and I'd like a career that matches my values. I can't imagine staying in one profession for the rest of my life just because it's the easier route.

Them: Why would you throw away a great salary for something you know nothing about?!

Your response: I've done my research and spoken to many people in the industry, and I'm confident I'll be able to get back to a healthy salary that I'm happy with within five years. For me that's worth the time investment to know I'd spend every day feeling more fulfilled.

Them: That can't be a real job, can it?

Your response: Yes, it is. I originally thought the same but it's something that people get paid for and happily enjoy, so I thought I'd give it a try.

Them: Are you sure you're making the right decision? How do you know if it will work out?

Your response: Truthfully, I don't know if it will! None of us really know what our future holds, but I'm excited to go on a career adventure. If it doesn't work out, I can always go back to what I know or follow a new passion.

CAREER COMEDOWN

Self-promotion is desperate

If you want to go in a new direction, self-promotion will be integral to your success. Until now you might have been in an industry where self-promotion wasn't really needed and, whilst you might feel more comfortable not doing it, now is the time to really embrace all the incredible benefits you can gain from it. As a 'self-promotion guru' (the title was given to me during my interview on BBC World News – lol), I have to give you this pep talk so you don't hide behind the 'I just don't do self-promotion' line and, instead, start embracing telling your story.

Choosing to twist is taking a gamble on yourself, so getting your narrative ready is essential for feeling confident to take on new environments. Having a clear self-promotion strategy will massively help you to convince people you can do what you say you can. I often like to remind people that instead of worrying about whether you'll look arrogant if you DO self-promote, you have to flip the perspective and question if it is more arrogant if you DON'T? Having zero self-promotion plans in place assumes that you're well known enough in a field to not have to promote yourself. I have no doubt you'll get to that point, but, until then, I encourage you to see this as something you could enjoy vs it feeling like a chore.

If you want to feel better about self-promoting, it can also help to change how you respond to other people self-promoting. By adopting a non-judgemental stance, we can quiet that inner critic, both internally and externally. Next time you see someone self-promoting why not change the script in your head to:

- *That's really brave that they shared that.*
- *I love that they had the courage to do that.*
- *I'm so grateful they shared that.*

- *I'm sure that will really help someone.*
- *It's amazing that they've secured that.*

Saying positive things about other people's storytelling will help you say more positive things to yourself when you do the same.

I'm starting from the bottom again

A career change is often seen as starting from scratch, but this perspective can limit growth and cloud the potential for meaningful transformation. Whilst it's true that some transitions require taking on lower-level roles, apprenticeships or even working for free to build experience in a new field, it's important to understand that these steps are not setbacks but investments. They might feel uncomfortable, especially if you consider yourself overqualified, but these roles bring you closer to the career you truly want.

Many people often overlook the fact that not all career changes require a complete reset. With the right approach, it's possible to reposition yourself in a way that makes the transition feel more adjacent as opposed to starting from scratch. Instead of focusing on the immediate discomfort, consider the long-term payoff. Three to five years of retraining or gaining new qualifications might feel a long time, but it's a short span in the context of a long working life. The potential reward, a job that brings passion, fulfilment and a sense of purpose, will almost always outweigh the dissatisfaction of staying in a career that drains your energy. A career change is not a failure; it's a realignment of your life's direction towards something more meaningful.

Now we've ditched those outdated outlooks, let's look at how you can positively shift your thinking during the twist process.

Mindset shift #1: You won't be perfect

In my first book I summarised people who delay their own progress in the pursuit of perfectionism, as 'Procrastinating Perfectionists'. If you are known to have a perfectionist complex, you will understand how much this can stunt your growth and why I don't want you to bring this mindset forward. When you are exploring something completely new, not only is it totally unrealistic to expect you to be perfect at it, but it's also not logical. You cannot be perfect at something you've never tried, so why set the bar so high? Of course, you will want to go out into the world with your best foot forward, but if you're waiting until you or someone else deems you to be perfect, you will be waiting an extremely long time and, worst-case scenario, may never take the leap.

When I was approached to write my first book my initial reaction was to say, 'Thanks but no thanks!' The truth is I'd never been celebrated as a writer, so I never in my wildest dreams thought that would be something I could do. Even when I had four different publishers approach me, I kept quickly shutting down the idea out of fear that I wasn't ready for it. Reflecting now, the things that helped me work through this and say yes to writing the first book were:

1. Putting aside my ego and realising I didn't have to be THE best (and that's okay!).
2. Reminding myself nobody was expecting me to be an expert; I could just be a contributor on the topic.

I remember saying to myself that if one person reads my book and gets a pay rise or leaves a toxic workplace, then that's all that matters. I didn't need to be a *Sunday Times* bestseller (which I wasn't, by the way), and I definitely didn't need to be perfect before I started.

I've since educated people on why it's important to adopt a 'Contributor vs Expert' mindset when you're starting something new. When I tell people they don't need to be an expert to get started, I see their shoulders instantly lower, their faces relax and the fear of needing to be the best fade away. Instead, I encourage people to just see themselves as a contributor to begin with. You are getting involved because you want to contribute to that topic or industry, you are not claiming to have all the answers and you're comfortable with not having them just yet. It's one of the most productive outlooks that will help you to start putting yourself out there without fear of judgement and unlock opportunities you didn't think were possible for yourself.

To the women reading this, I'm especially speaking to you. If you haven't heard of *The Confidence Gap* study, it shows that women are more likely to underestimate their abilities, whilst men tend to overestimate theirs.[2] It's a tough truth, but it's one that needs to be addressed. Women often feel they need to be 100 per cent competent before they can feel confident. This can hold us back from jumping into opportunities where we could thrive, simply because we're waiting for that perfect moment when we feel fully prepared. But the more you show up for yourself, use your voice and let yourself be seen (polished or not polished), the more benefits you will see.

Mindset shift #2: Your confidence won't be consistent

It is extremely important for me to say that if you are twisting, there will absolutely be times where you feel the itch to run back to what you know – especially when things get tough, or you don't see immediate results. Humans like comfort, stability and knowing that our efforts will pay off, and twisting, unfortunately, does not guarantee any of that. Questioning your decision and yourself is completely normal, and will likely happen on a regular basis. Having been through this myself and watched so many friends go through the same thing, I named the experience 'Pre-launch fear' (PLF). Pre-launch fear is that gut-churning feeling you get right before you're about to do something brave, like sending off that dream job application, or sharing that podcast episode you've spent hours editing and perfecting. Not only will you question if you are good enough to go for it, but your brain starts dredging up all kinds of irrelevant things that have *nothing* to do with your success.

Let me give you an example. A friend of mine was about to launch a coaching programme, and twenty-four hours before she hit 'go', she sent me a voice note listing all the reasons why she was crazy to think it would work, even referencing things like the fact she was single or didn't own her home as evidence it wouldn't work. I remember listening to it and thinking, 'WHAT is she even talking about?!' None of that had anything to do with her ability to crush it with her coaching programme (which she totally did, by the way). I reminded her that none of those thoughts should stop her from trying and that if she wanted people to believe in her, she needed to believe in herself. If you ever feel that PLF creeping in, just know that it's totally normal to have doubts when you're backing yourself, especially in something new. It doesn't mean you've made a huge mistake or that you should run back to a career that wasn't fulfilling you, it just means you have to keep reminding yourself why you're doing what you're doing.

Mindset shift #3: You don't have to figure it out alone

Being fiercely independent can have many positives in life, but when you're changing directions or starting something new, it's better to get help from others than struggle on alone. Whether you don't like asking for help or you're trying to prove to people this is the right decision, isolating yourself is a recipe for disaster. I know far too many people who have taken this route and found themselves with damaged confidence and reaching burnout far quicker than they ever anticipated. So, I want you to know a few things:

- More people want to say yes than you think.
- People don't know how to help you if you don't tell them.
- It's still your story and success even if other people contribute to it.
- No amount of proving yourself is worth damaging your health for.
- You're not the only person going through the experience.
- You can go fast alone but far with others.
- No one is expecting you to have all the answers.

No one will ever look at your career twist and say: 'They only got there because they asked people to support them through the process, what a cop out.' The most successful people in the world are not the ones who claim to have figured out every obstacle alone. They are the people who knew their strengths, knew their weaknesses and knew how to get the support they needed to move forward.

Changing Lanes

So now we've gone through the emotions you might be feeling, the behaviours you need to unlearn and the mindset shifts you need to adopt, let's start talking about the next best steps to give yourself the freedom to explore something new.

Test-drive your next chapter

If you've ever bought a new car, you've probably been for a test drive. Before you hand over a big chunk of money, it's important that you feel confident in what you're buying and that you have the chance to spot any potential snags or issues that might cause you problems later. Where possible, you should do the same in your career – especially if it's something you've never done before.

The thing that has probably stopped you from going for it until now is that age old question – How will I know it will all work out? – and time. Whether it's your crammed schedule, your childcare responsibilities, or your lack of motivation because you're hating every minute of your current role, we need to find some ways to claw back some time and reinvest it into your new direction. It will continue to feel like an unachievable option if you don't create time to try out what this next career could look like.

Test-driving your new career could involve:

- Volunteering in industry-related communities or charities to get a sense of the type of people you could be working with.
- Offering to do free work for prospective clients or customers (these could even be friends or family who meet your prospect criteria).

- Starting a side hustle to experiment with business models.
- Attending industry-relevant events to learn more about the field and meet new connections.
- Taking on part-time or weekend shifts in your new area.
- Working on the type of daily activities you might be doing if you took the leap (posting on social media, creating proposals, pitching to people).
- Partaking in training that gives you real-work experience or scenarios to practise.

The more you can experience your new direction, the more you can go into the decision feeling like it was the right choice. So now I want you to think about:

- What things would help you to feel confident about career twisting?
- When could you claw back time to invest in your future?
- What changes do you need to make to protect that time?

Chase the passion not the profit

I know this might sound idealistic but stick with me on this. When I first started F*ck Being Humble, I didn't set out with an ambition to set up a giant company, nor did I set serious goals or targets. I was exploring the industry: building up my public speaking profile, growing a network of my own and creating an event experience that filled a gap in the market. It was a passion project, not even a side hustle, because there was no business plan in place; I didn't know I needed to register the company name on Companies House or consider that I would definitely need an accountant. Whilst it might not sound very business savvy, it was this naivety that made the first year of growing F*ck Being Humble so enjoyable. I had a full-time job that paid for my living costs and so I could enjoy the process without the constant dread of underdelivering or feeling like my whole livelihood was riding on it. Chasing my passion and building it on my own terms helped me get really clear on what I was drawn to, and, just as importantly, what I definitely didn't want to do. So, when I was finally ready to take the plunge and go full time with the business, I wasn't stretched thin trying to offer every possible service under the sun – I knew exactly what I wanted to focus on.

Chasing passion over profit is not always easy. I spoke to Kyle, a major foodie and kitchen expert, who chose to leave his marketing job to pursue a career as a chef. He immediately loved the move, but soon found the toll of the physical labour and the salary limitations too difficult to sustain. After six months, he made the difficult decision to go back into marketing, though felt miserable and defeated. 'I lay in bed thinking about cooking,' he told me. 'I don't lay in bed thinking about marketing.' After eighteen months of working in marketing again, he decided to give his dream another go. This time around, he managed to secure a fixed role with a salary he was comfortable with and reignited his love for his career. I share this story because Kyle's career comedown came from pursuing his dream career and then having to abandon it because of the limited financial trajectory. But as we discussed in the audit chapter, life is about trade-offs and, for Kyle, happiness and creativity at work ended up being the number one priority. And it wasn't just Kyle who had a spring in his step; his partner told me how much happier she was to see him excited about work again. Whether we realise it or not, we often forget that chasing profit over happiness can actually seep into our relationships too. So, when you're thinking about twisting, keep asking yourself what the costs of your decisions are.

Speak to people who are doing it

If you can't try before you change, at least speak to people who are doing what you want to do. There is no better insight into a role than actually speaking to those who are in the trenches, either where you want to be or a few steps ahead of you. I remember coming up with (what I thought was) an incredible idea for an app and wanted to reach out to a few app founders in my network before I got too far down the line. I got on a call with a trusted connection who has successfully launched and runs a brilliant app in the creative industry, and within minutes of us chatting, she gave me such helpful insider advice. She loved my idea, but she also said:

- Be prepared to work with a lot of technical people.
- Be prepared for data / GDPR / and fixing bugs to be your life.
- Be prepared to build a team (unless you have technical skills – which I didn't).
- Be prepared to invest a lot of money and continue to need more money.

She wasn't trying to put me off, but she wanted me to really ask myself: 'Is this what I actually want?' And honestly, it didn't take long for me to realise that the reality of turning this 'nice' idea into something real wasn't exactly what I saw myself doing, or even enjoying, on a daily basis. It was just one of those many ideas I had and, when I looked at how I wanted my schedule to feel, I knew this one wasn't something I was ready to chase. I'm so grateful for that conversation and for all the others I've had since then. If you're feeling unsure or are looking for more clarity before jumping in, I highly recommend you do the same. One of my top pieces of advice when it comes to learning from others' experiences is to be strategic with your sampling. When you're reaching out to people to learn about their experiences, make sure you're connecting with those who are:

1. **New players and seasoned players**. Someone who is just starting out might have a different perspective to someone who has been in the industry you're trying to crack for a long time. You can learn heaps from both – and neither is necessarily better than the other – but it's helpful that you keep in mind what career stage someone is at when processing their advice. For example, new players can give you a valuable, up-to-date insight into what it takes to break into an industry, whilst the veterans are better placed to give you an overarching idea of how the industry has grown or changed overtime.
2. **Career stickers and career twisters**. If you speak to a midwife who stumbled into their role, you'll likely get a different account of what's working in the industry than if you chat to someone who quit their corporate job to do something more meaningful. When you're getting their input, ask people what led them to their career and how they measure success.
3. **Norm-followers and path-carvers**. Thinking about growing a business? Speak to someone who went down the investment and building a team route vs the solopreneurs on how their experiences differ and which feels most appealing to you.

Do your desk research

If you're not able to speak to someone personally about their experience, go and listen to podcasts about people building their businesses or changing career directions. Podcasts are one of my absolute favourite places to research markets, jobs or new roles – I know from speaking on many that they are a great resource too for developing a deeper understanding of almost any topic. You get the real, unpolished stuff, where speakers are honest about their struggles, wins and the decisions they've made along the way. They're free, easy to access and you can learn a ton from other people's highs and lows before you make a twist in your own career.

Podcasts I've found useful on my journey are:

- *The High Performance*
- *How I Built This*
- *Ladies Who Launch*
- *Dare To Lead*

Plan your exit strategy

Before you depart any situation, I want you to get the most out of it. Go on training days to brush up your presenting skills? Yes. Finally get those testimonials you've been meaning to ask for from your clients? Yes. Go collect the results from a recent project to better sell you for future opportunities? Yes, yes, yes. I want you to think about what will help you when you eventually twist that you can be preparing now. The more ammunition you're armed with for your next chapter the more confident you'll be feeling on day one. Here is a list of things I'd recommend everyone does as they start out:

Positive testimonials

I know it can feel like a bit of a hassle and maybe even a little uncomfortable, but trust me, positive testimonials are gold because they act as social proof that what you're saying about yourself is legit. I always give the example that Nike can tell you they're the best at making trainers, but if a hundred other people are backing that up, you're much more likely to believe it, right? The same goes for you. So, when you're gathering testimonials, I want you to provide prompts and questions that will position you for your next opportunity in the best possible way. If you're moving from a finance job into the wellness world, for instance, it's not about how great you are at crunching numbers. I want to hear about your communication skills, your calming presence and your ability to connect with people.

If you're struggling to know where to start, I'd recommend getting the job specification for the industry you are applying for and highlighting all the key skills they are looking for. Then, come up with questions that help your referrer speak to those skills. I'll give you extra points if you can get the person who's giving the testimonial to leave it as a LinkedIn recommendation. If you're wondering if it's worth it, according to LinkedIn's 2025 Global Hiring Trends Report, 79 per cent of recruiters consider recommendations to be a significant factor in their hiring decisions and Jobvite found that 70 per cent of hiring managers trust recommendations from LinkedIn connections more than traditional references.[3] I know it sounds like a bit of work upfront, but once it's done, it will save you so much time down the road. Plus, it's way easier to get these referrals whilst you're still working with someone, rather than after you've already moved on and they're no longer on your radar.

Collect data

When we looked at sticking in your career, we discussed the importance of being able to connect your performance and contributions back to company goals and metrics. The same principle is important for twisting. The more data and insights you have that demonstrate what you can deliver, the easier it will be to build trust with people in your next role, even if the industries are completely different. Examples of this might be:

- The project helped increase revenue by 40 per cent.
- The website update led to double the website traffic the previous year.
- The copyrighting strategy increased the email-open rate and click-through rate to . . .
- We created a downloadable report that had over 500 downloads from businesses that include . . .

Along with the data, try to gather any visual references or examples that might be useful for websites, portfolios or social media posting in the future, as it will save you having to recreate them (especially if you're not very design-focused!).

Get the referrals

For those of you going solo or setting up a company, I want you to ask for introductions and referrals. One of the hardest things of 'funemployment' is not knowing where to find a job, a client or your first customer; referrals definitely yield more than cold calling/emailing and can help take some of the anxiety out of the process. It's always more useful to ask people for a specific introduction rather than a vague 'keep an eye out for me'. For example, saying something like 'I saw you were connected with Michelle Walters at Microsoft. Would you be open to introducing us on email as I'd love to arrange a coffee with her' will always be more effective than a generic request to share something around their network.

Remember, the other person is well within their rights to say no and, likelihood is, you'll receive many rejections along the way. But if you get in the habit of asking, you'll eventually see doors of opportunity open up.

Leave on a high

Sometimes, when you've had a really tough time in your job and you're ready to walk out the door, it can feel like you just want to set the whole place on fire and never look back. Trust me, I get it. But industries can be surprisingly small and you never know when someone from your past job might be in a position to help you further down the road. Now, I'm not saying you should force fake friendships in your final weeks, but it's definitely worth thinking about leaving on a positive note, or 'finishing well' as I like to call it. What I mean by that is offering up support, having coffees and chats with people, replying to all company emails, or sending updates about your next venture to contacts that could help you on your journey in the future. I know some of you might have experienced that awkward 'freeze out' where you suddenly find yourself being excluded or barely spoken to after handing in your notice. If that's the case, I totally get how tempting it is to check out early, but try to push through. Whether you need them now or later, you never know when these contacts might be able to support you. Leave with your head held high and dignity intact.

Your safety budget

Your safety budget is the secret weapon that gives you the freedom to walk away from any career on your own terms. If there's one piece of advice I wish I'd gotten sooner, it's to start building that fund before you actually need it. I completely recognise that it's not always easy to put money aside every month, especially when in the middle of a financial crisis, but if it is possible for you to build that cushion, then you absolutely should be prioritising it. Often people find themselves locked into jobs they don't want because they are so dependent on the paycheque that it feels impossible to leave, despite knowing it's the right time to go. Even if you've got a solid plan for what's next, life doesn't always play out perfectly. You might face an employment gap, or if you're self-employed, you could have months with big earnings and others with . . . well, no earnings. Having that buffer gives you the freedom to choose when you leave, rather than being forced to stay out of necessity. Trust me, it's all about having that extra peace of mind, so you can move on your terms, not because you feel stuck.

Things that can help with this:
1. **Set a clear goal on how much you need.** The amount you need to save really depends on your goals and how much disposable income you have after covering your bills, or how much time you have to save. At the very least, it's a good idea to aim for three to six months' worth of expenses. This gives you more freedom to make your next move without financial stress, or even invest in yourself as you transition. If you're planning on taking a longer break between jobs to figure out your next step, you might want to aim for a full year's worth of savings. That way, you can

explore new opportunities without worrying about money holding you back. There's no one-size-fits-all when it comes to this, and ultimately, you've got to do what's right for your own timings, what you can afford to save and how much you think you need to cover yourself. But if you set a clear goal, you're way more likely to stay on track.

2. **Do a spending audit.** After speaking to a lot of people who took significant pay cuts to follow their passion, the general feedback I got was they realised they needed less than they thought. Whether it's swapping the store-bought lunches for a packed lunch, reducing the frequency of your beauty treatments or cutting down how many TV subscriptions you commit to, think about the spending decisions that could be put on hold as you do some saving. Small changes like sharing a Spotify account or opting for jogs in the park instead of a pricey gym membership can add up to save you hundreds of pounds a year. The goal isn't to completely deprive yourself, but to think about the little things you can put on hold whilst you focus on building that cushion. Once you see how much you can save, it can be empowering and might even help you realise you're perfectly happy with less – you can always reintroduce things you've cut into your budget at a later date.

3. **Automate your savings**. Full confession: I'm *terrible* at saving. I'm the kind of person who lives in the moment and, honestly, I didn't really get serious about saving until I got engaged and started dreaming up my Pinterest-perfect wedding. At that point, I was 31 and wishing I had taken saving more seriously in my twenties! The best thing I ever

did for myself was setting up automatic transfers so that a chunk of money left my account every time I got paid. I didn't have to think about it, and I certainly didn't have to fight the temptation to spend it or tell myself, 'I'll do it next month.' Once I started this, I saved up WAY more than I ever had before. If you're just starting, don't worry about going big right away, you can start small. Even saving £10–20 a month can really add up over time. You'll see that little pot grow and feel like you're actually making progress towards your goal. The key is consistency, and automation takes the guesswork (and temptation) out of the equation.

4. **Create something to sell in the short term**. When Tyler the Creator first launched his t-shirt collection, he couldn't afford the fancy dyes for screen-printing, so he made do with cheaper iron-on transfers. Fast forward a bit, and after selling those lower-budget t-shirts, he was able to save up enough to buy the more expensive dyes and create the higher-quality products he had originally planned to. In his words: 'Everything is figure-out-able. It just depends on if you have the energy to put in.' Your first step doesn't have to be perfect, or even the long-term solution. It could be something small, like offering out-of-hours consultancy to small businesses or selling clothes you no longer wear on second-hand platforms. Whatever it is, every little bit adds up.

For those of you with limited time, creating passive income could be the way to go. For example, let's say you create a guide teaching people how to use LinkedIn effectively. It might take some upfront time, but the beauty is that, once it's created, it's yours to sell without extra effort. In the summer of 2020, just a few months into running F*ck Being Humble full time, I started offering CV reviews. I offered them at £20 for an hour and within a week of promoting I had 40 bookings. Was it exhausting and a bit monotonous? Yes. But was it worth it for what I had to invest in myself? Absolutely. Whether it's something you enjoy or not, there's always money to be made, you just need to find what works for you.

5. **Don't be afraid of crowdfunding investments.** If you're wanting to launch something that might require some upfront investment, crowdfunding might be something to explore. It lets you gather money from a bunch of people instead of relying on things like bank loans or venture capital, which can be tough to get, especially for new or unconventional ideas. If the campaign doesn't reach its goal, you can reassess and refine your approach without losing personal funds. Plus, a successful campaign doesn't just raise money, it shows there's real demand for your idea – validation that can lead to even more support and investment down the road. The Year Here program, which inspires entrepreneurs to tackle social problems, actually recommends that participants kick things off by hosting a 'Friends and Family' crowdbacker event. This could be a Zoom call or an in-person gathering, where you invite everyone you know to pitch in whatever they can. It might be just £10 or £20 – but if 40 people contribute, that's £400 in the bank. I know that these ideas can sound scary, but as I've already stated, choosing to twist is choosing to leave your comfort zone. So, instead of hiding behind the fear of the unknown, ask yourself:

What can I do right now to set myself up for success in this next chapter? Crowdfunding could be the perfect first step.

TOP TIPS: *I spoke to Emmanuel Asuquo, qualified financial advisor and TV presenter committed to supporting both individuals and corporate clients in gaining financial freedom, and he recommended three top tips to create a more financially fruitful self:*

Go where people value you: 'It is so important to be in the right environment. When I worked in finance, I never felt like I belonged and so I always had to search for validity. Your skills in the wrong environment are going to feel like a curse, but your skills in the right environment are going to feel like a blessing. I realised I needed to put the skills I'm really good at in the right environment as opposed to me putting myself in a place where the things I'm really good at were not appreciated. When I worked at different banks, they didn't appreciate me, but when I launched myself on social media, they wanted to pay me to do content for them. I had to put my skills in the right environment for it to be appreciated.'

Always be upskilling: 'From a skills perspective, you need to be doing personal development and upskilling to command higher salaries. What additional things can you do to be more valuable in the workplace? And how can you make sure that if your company lets you go, other companies will want you? What skills are you adding to yourself? What things are you doing that other people are not doing that makes you rare? It's really important to consistently upskill yourself at all times so that if you find yourself in the job market, you are a desirable candidate.'

Know that you are the value: 'The biggest thing I needed to do was to love myself. Coming from a council estate and poor background, when it came to spending money, I would recklessly buy lots of things. It took me a while to understand that the car I drove was valuable because I was the one driving it, rather than it giving me any value itself. I'm not going to allow the world to dictate how much I'm worth – I want to dictate that for myself.'

The art of being a beginner again

In my eyes, no one is ever too established to try something new. We can all go back to square one and dive into things that might feel uncomfortable or totally outside our usual lane. It's probably going to be tough at first, but do you want your tombstone to say, 'Quit career to try something new but was too scared to actually do it'? I don't think so. You're better than that. The reality is, when you're starting over, you'll probably have to do stuff you don't love, stuff you're bad at, and sometimes you'll have to do it in front of other people. (Cringe, I know.) But guess what? Years from now, you'll look back and think, 'I'm really glad I tried that, even though I was horrible at it, it taught me so much about where to focus my energy.' And that, my friend, is growth. I also like to think about how my bravery might inspire others. We're so worried about the negative things people might say that we forget how our willingness to try could actually be the thing that lights a fire under someone else. Maybe they need to see someone else being real and vulnerable to take that first step themselves. You can either quietly work behind the scenes, or you can bring people along for the ride and let their support fuel your journey. Either way, don't let fear of judgement stop you from doing something that could change your life, and maybe even someone else's too.

Push through the silence

Whether it's applying for jobs or promoting your offering on LinkedIn, I want you to remember that just because people aren't vocal doesn't mean they're not impressed. This is a lesson I've learned through my own journey building my business, and it's something you should keep in mind the next time you're feeling like you're not getting the response you hoped for. On Alice Benhams' podcast *Starting the Conversation* she interviewed Danielle Wallington, the founder of Flock Here, about her journey of raising £18,000 for her app and community.[4] On the show she shared: 'You never know who is watching. Even if you're sick of talking about something you're probably not talking about it enough. It's about pushing past the discomfort until you get to a stage where you just don't care because you know that talking about it enough is going to get you to where you need to be.' With this strategy, her crowdfunding campaign received a huge surge in contributions during the final hours of it being open, as people she hadn't realised were paying attention suddenly showed up in a big way. So don't assume that just because people aren't publicly praising you or opening doors for you right away, they aren't impressed. Trust me, they are. They just might show their support at different points.

When you're going through a reinvention, persistence and grit are going to be your best friends. There will be moments when it feels like no one's listening or noticing, and you'll start questioning whether this new path is the right one. But you can't give up when things get tough, you have to keep believing in the new version of yourself even when the results aren't immediate. Take someone like Oprah Winfrey, for instance. Early in her career, she was told she was 'unfit for television' and even got fired from her first TV job as a news anchor. But instead of letting that define her, she persisted, honed her skills and created the iconic *Oprah Winfrey Show*. Had she given up after those setbacks, she wouldn't have become the global media mogul she is today. The key takeaway? Don't let a few setbacks or lack of immediate response discourage you. Keep pushing forward, and eventually, your persistence will pay off.

Talk about all your experiences

Even if your past work experience doesn't seem directly related to what you're doing now, it's still worth talking about. You never know who might hear your story and realise how those 'random' roles you've had actually bring a fresh perspective to the table. The skills you've picked up, whether it's problem-solving, communication, leadership or project management, are all transferable. They show that you can adapt and think outside the box, so don't be shy about the journey you've been on – embrace it. It makes you stand out, and that's exactly what you want when you're in reinvention mode. I specifically remember working at one company where my colleague to the left of me had worked on some of the coolest shows on MTV and my colleague to the right of me had worked on epic projects with the UN. But neither of them told me about this until about six months into my time at the business, so, for the longest time, I only knew them by their job titles, not by their amazing backgrounds. Not only did learning about them help us to build better relationships, but it also led to much more exciting collaborations. You never know who might appreciate your experience, even if it feels 'unrelated' to what you're doing now. Don't, therefore, get caught up in that nonsense about not having enough 'relevant' experience yet. Own your journey, because the skills and stories you've picked up along the way could open doors in ways you can't even imagine.

The Power Of Strong Support Systems

We've already talked about how important it is to speak to people before making a career twist, but now I want to emphasise why it's just as important to have the right support throughout your journey. Over the years I've learned that just as you can't expect one job role to complete you, you also can't expect one group of people to understand all of your career decisions and automatically know how to best support you through them. One of the best pieces of advice I ever got was: 'The people on your front row can and will change throughout the different decades of your life.' And that's totally okay. People come into your life for a reason, but they don't always need to be there for your next career move. Never be afraid to expand your circle and seek out people who are more closely aligned with your new path.

In fact, in 1973, Stanford sociologist Mark Granovetter released a theory that weak ties – casual connections and loose acquaintances – were actually more helpful than strong ones in securing employment. Your weak ties connect you in networks outside of your circle, whereas strong ties (your closest friends or supporters) will most likely already have the same connections you have or have helped you as far as they can. When we're busy or pressed for time, it's easy to default to spending time with people we know well, but I've also gained so much value from connecting with my weak ties. I'm talking about people who I may have met once at an event or one time commented on their LinkedIn posts. Almost every time, these conversations have led to something unexpected, with new introductions, opportunities and ideas that I couldn't have predicted.

So when I say make time for *everyone*, I don't mean stretching yourself thin or sacrificing your well-being. I mean being open to meeting and engaging with as many people as possible, even if you can't picture them being your best friend that you go on holidays with. It's much better to have too many people in your corner than not enough. Here are some questions to reflect on:

- Who is someone you could reconnect with?
- Who is someone you have connected with digitally but not in real life?
- Who is someone you offered to grab coffee with but never did?

Find people who get *why* you're doing what you're doing

A few months before quitting my job, I was lucky enough to find two incredible women, Daisy and Poonam, who from the outset got what I was doing. We'd met through a few of my events and, when we realised we were all running small businesses with similar models and facing the same frustrations and obstacles, we created a WhatsApp group that became my lifeline. It was a safe space to vent, ask questions and get feedback during a really uncertain time.

One thing we did to keep going during such a tough time was to celebrate the small wins. Every Friday, we'd do a check-in via voice notes in our group called 'Wins Before Dins' and we'd share two or three things we'd accomplished that week that we were proud of. It didn't have to be big: anything from getting ready before noon, setting a boundary, eating well, landing a new client or sticking to a social media post streak. These weekly check-ins became a ritual we looked forward to, and they did wonders for our confidence and perseverance. There was no sense of competition, and none of us ever felt like we couldn't relate to the others' struggles. We were all in it together, lifting each other up, and I honestly don't think I'd be where I am today without having their support. If I can urge you to do anything, it's to find two to three people that you really trust that you could create this safety net with.

Here are some more questions to reflect on:

- What type of people do you need on your front row right now?
- What do you want them to understand about your journey?
- Where might you find these people?
- Who might be able to introduce you?

Find people to help you get ahead

One of my all-time favourite TED talks is by Carla Harris, and it's called *How to Find the People to Help You Get Ahead at Work*.[5] In it, she talks about two types of currency in our careers: performance currency and relationship currency. Performance currency is the one we're all familiar with – it's about showing up, doing your job well and building credibility through your output. It's the currency we tend to focus on the most, constantly looking for validation and proving our worth. But relationship currency is just as important, if not more so. It's all about building connections with people so that when you're not in the room, others will advocate for you. It's about creating a network that speaks highly of you, even when you're not around to speak for yourself. As soon as I heard this, I immediately thought of all the times I dismissed building relationships with people because they weren't 'my kind of people'. I used to joke, 'If I wouldn't grab cocktails with them after work, why bother making the effort?' Now, looking back on my career, I can honestly say it's one of my biggest regrets. I want to be clear this isn't about being transactional or fake. It's about understanding who could open doors for you or speak highly of you in spaces where you can thrive.

Everyone should be thinking about who can help them get ahead at work. The good news is that these people don't need to be right next to you at your office. They can be mentors, peers or even superfans of your work. Having these people in your corner will seriously increase the positive opportunities that come your way. And just like it helps, as I mentioned earlier, Nike to have one hundred customers raving about their products to build social proof, the more people who are championing you, the easier it is to reinvent yourself in a new industry. So, start thinking about who you want in your corner and put in the effort to build that relationship currency. It'll pay off in ways you can't even imagine.

Reflect on these questions:

- Who holds influence in your company or industry?
- Who has a network that you might be able to benefit from?
- Are these people in your existing network?
- If not, where can you go to find them?

Find people who are great at the things you're bad at

This is one of those things that often gets overlooked, but I truly believe it's something everyone should focus on (whether you're changing careers or not). As we've already discussed, you're going to feel like a constant beginner when you're stepping into something new, and it's easy to want to surround yourself with people who share your interests and think like you. Whilst that's great for building friendships and emotional support, it's not always the best strategy when you're trying to get ahead in a new career direction. If you really want to make progress, you need to get clear on where you feel out of your depth and then find people who can help guide you through those areas. A great support system isn't just about emotional support or having people who 'get' you, it's also about connecting with people who have the skills or expertise you need to fill in the gaps you're struggling with.

Take one of my friends, for example. She's been unsure whether to keep pushing forward with her business or just walk away. When we dug into what kind of support she really needed, it became clear she wasn't looking for someone to just cheer her on, she desperately needed a sales expert who could help her find new opportunities in a way that felt true to her. She had spent years building relationships within her industry but hadn't focused on finding the right people to guide her where she needed it most.

So, I want you to ask yourself, what do you really need help with? What are your blind spots? Make sure the people in your corner can fill those gaps, even if it means stepping outside your usual circle. Trust me, it'll make a world of difference.

- What are the weak spots you need help with?
- What knowledge or experience do you worry is lacking that might hold you back?
- Do you know anyone who could help you with this?

Find people who aren't afraid of moving on

It's not just about having people who get why you're doing what you're doing, it's also about having people who will be real with you. You need people who aren't afraid to give you a reality check, who will help you self-reflect and ask the tough questions. People who will ask you, 'Are you sure you really want this? Is this still the path that lights you up?' Sometimes we get so caught up in our own journey that we need someone outside of ourselves to remind us that it's okay to pivot, and even more importantly, it's okay to walk away when something isn't right.

In one interview, I spoke to Sophie Rogozinska, a career twister, who shared a story about a friend of hers who had no problem moving from one job to another. She was a free-spirited soul who saw job-hopping as an exciting opportunity rather than a failure. For Sophie, having a friend like this was incredibly refreshing. It wasn't about sticking to one thing at all costs; it was about following your passions, embracing change and being open to the fact that it's okay to leave something behind if it's not working anymore.

The best thing about reinventing yourself is that it doesn't need be one and done. Just because you're choosing a new path now doesn't mean it's your final destination. Life's too short to stay in something that doesn't fit anymore, and sometimes the best thing you can do is give yourself permission to move on, regroup and try something new. You don't have to get it perfect on the first try. The people who truly care about you will encourage you to keep evolving and will support you when it's time to switch gears, reminding you that each reinvention is part of the process of getting closer to who you're meant to be. So, surround yourself with those who won't hesitate to tell you when it's time to move on, so you can keep evolving, no matter how many times it takes.

Repositioning Yourself

So far in this chapter we've talked about test-driving your new direction, getting the most from your exit strategy, why you shouldn't fear being a beginner again, and how important networks will be to help you move through your journey with confidence. Now I want to help you with some practical steps to hit the ground running and make sure you don't second guess yourself or hold yourself back. If you want to reinvent yourself, you need to reposition how people see you. Throughout my career in advertising, I worked with many businesses on how to rebrand themselves to reach a new audience and, whilst running F*ck Being Humble, I advised thousands of people on how to pitch themselves to the external world.

So, let's look at some of the essential things that will set you up for success:

Reframe your past and present

One of the questions that comes up time and time again when people are trying to reinvent themselves in their careers, is: 'How do I talk about my past experience and make it relevant?' If you've worked in investment banking and you're pivoting into becoming a therapist, you're going to need to make some edits to your career history. Don't worry, you don't need to scrap anything, but you might need to spin your story slightly differently:

1. **Find the parallels:** Writing a CV or application for a completely new industry can definitely feel a little intimidating, but the trick is to focus on your transferable skills. The first thing I want you to do is find a job listing that sparks your interest and highlight everything you've already got experience in. Don't think too literally – think instead about how your existing skills can be applied in a new way. Let's take the investment banker wanting to pivot into therapy example. Whilst you might not have been a therapist before, think about moments when you've had to listen closely, problem-solve or handle tough conversations. You could also highlight your achievements – maybe you led a team through a big project, or introduced strategies that boosted employee retention. By framing your experience around your strengths, you're showing how your past roles have prepped you to succeed in a fresh environment. This way, potential employers will see the value you bring, no matter where your career has taken you.

2. **Strip out industry-specific words:** When you're making a leap into a new industry or role, one of the best things you can do is remove any industry-specific jargon from your CV or LinkedIn profile. Sure, the terminology might feel like second nature to you, but it can unintentionally highlight the fact that you don't have direct experience in the new field. For example, investment bankers might want to remove terms like 'mergers' and 'IPOs'. Or if you're a marketing manager dreaming of becoming a chef, phrases like 'A/B testing' and 'click-through

rates' probably won't get much attention in a kitchen. To make sure you're speaking the right language, take some time to research the companies or industries you're targeting, check out their websites, sign up for their newsletters and dive into their social media. The more you can match their language and vibe, the more likely they are to open their doors to you.

3. **Hobbies and interests:** In some scenarios, you can't always embellish your past work experience to perfectly align with your new path, but you can fill in any gaps with your hobbies and interests. A lot of people overlook this when writing their CV or putting together their portfolio, but I want you to think of them as the bridge between where you've been and where you're going. If you're moving into a marketing role, mentioning that you've been honing your skills by doing personal branding projects outside of work or have read over 100 marketing books can show your commitment and passion for the industry, without needing to fake expertise. Or if your dream is to move into real estate, you might include that you love going to networking events to develop your relationship-building skills and travelling to new neighbourhoods and cities to better understand how to promote locations. These examples don't only give you something tangible to talk about but also demonstrate that you're proactive and invested in your new direction, making you a more compelling candidate.

Soft launch yourself

How do you go from talking about one area to another confidently? Something I recommend is to soft launch yourself.

CAREER COMEDOWN

The phrase 'soft launch' has been widely used to describe celebrities who slowly reveal hints of a new romantic relationship on social media, before they're ready to commit to the official announcement – a 'hard launch'. And it's a trend that I recommend my followers do when they want to start posting online about a new subject area, but they're scared to make the first move. Your fear of sharing usually stems from having a pre-existing network or group of people who know you as one specific thing, and you're worried they might question why you're chiming up on this new topic all of a sudden.

Let's take my friend Ella, a London-based DJ, who had been sharing highlights of her playing at club nights but hadn't yet shared content of her speaking to camera about her love of the music industry. She was worried people would judge her if she started recommending playlists or talking about her job opportunities because it would feel out of the blue, unexpected or like she was claiming to be a 'know-it-all' on the topic. I recommended that she could soft launch herself on social media to pre-empt and frame what she wanted shared with her network, so they knew what to expect. Using a collection of personal and professional video clips, she created montage video with a voiceover where she introduced herself, what motivates her, what content she was planning on sharing and why. This made Ella feel more comfortable to start self-promoting because she was able to influence why she was sharing before she actually did. I've seen people write articles on 'Why after 10 years I'm moving from a job in finance to being a carpenter' as a way to educate and share the change with their network. The goal is to give a 'warm-up' update, before you officially hard launch yourself in the new industry you want to be a part of.

Become obsessed with your new industry

If you've ever tuned in to *Dragon's Den* or *Shark Tank*, you've probably noticed that the investors don't just invest in ideas, they invest in the people behind them. They look for hunger, determination, passion and dedication because they know, whilst skills can be taught, those things can't. If you want to give yourself the best shot at making a strong impression in your next step, I highly recommend you get obsessed with your new world and are able to demonstrate that. (Okay, not obsessed to the point where you're losing sleep over it, but you know what I mean – make your passion undeniable.)

For example, when I first realised I wanted to work in advertising, I started writing a blog about my favourite ad campaigns. It was definitely not my best work – honestly, it's hidden somewhere deep in the internet now – but it helped me figure out what I truly loved about the industry. With every post, I was analysing what worked and what didn't, and offering my own suggestions on how things could be better. And whilst not many people engaged with it (and by not many I mean no one) I wasn't doing it for likes. It was a tool to help reposition myself. I was able to mention it when I applied for jobs, finding that it was an effective conversation starter that showcased my genuine interest in the field. If you're not into writing, you can get more involved in your new industry by listening to relevant podcasts, reading up on the latest topical books, watching documentaries or films that explore your field, making time to visit exhibitions, or even picking up new hobbies that demonstrate the skills you need in the new role. Here are some more ways you can show your passion convincingly:

New career	Ways to throw yourself into that industry
Nutritionist	- Attending wellness events - Making your own recipes - Taking part in exercise challenges - Watching documentaries on the latest or old food trends
Teacher	- Volunteer to work with children in your local community - Read books that explore different communication styles - Take part in activity-based workshops to study teaching approaches
Writer	- Host a book club - Subscribe to industry publications - Set yourself a reading challenge - Write a Substack

Everything we've been exploring in this section is about encouraging you to embody your new career, so that you don't doubt that you deserve to be there. Remember, if you want to be known as something, you need to believe that's what you are.

Stop doing the same as everyone else

You might not want to hear this, but, when you're applying for new opportunities, you're going to be up against some folks who have more experience than you, which means you'll need to get a little more creative in how you stand out. We've already talked about the importance of self-promotion, but now let's take it up a notch and explore all the ways you can show people you're worth taking a chance on. There are of course all the usual avenues for applying to jobs – emails, recruiters, etc. – but if you want to grab attention, you need to do something that cuts through the noise.

In October 2023, when I decided to take my leap and raise awareness for the 'F*ck Being Humble' movement in the US, I wanted to make an impact in my dream city, New York. I could've done the usual introductory meetings to build my profile, but they didn't feel big enough to make me stand out. So, I grabbed a couple of fold-out chairs, put up a sandwich board that read 'Free Career Advice', and set up shop in Washington Square Park, one of New York's busiest park spots. The first twenty minutes were tough. I sat there thinking, 'Why is no one coming? Was this a terrible idea? Why did I not prepare for this?!' But then, slowly and surely, people came and sat down, and as the day progressed a small queue formed. I documented the whole thing and shared it online, and that video ended up going viral. Not only did it have a great online reaction but it also led to paid opportunities with brands and communities who loved the idea and who wanted to help me to bring it to life. The point I'm trying to make is that no one asked me to do this and it's definitely not the traditional way to line up clients or partnerships. But this wasn't just about raising awareness for my business, it was about showcasing who I am as a brand. When people saw the activation, they used words like courage, bravery and generosity to describe it. It raised awareness of who I was, what I was about and the type of person I am to work with.

The same idea of thinking outside the box applies to others I've seen in action, like the person who stood in Canary Wharf,

London, with a life-size CV on an A1 board that said 'HIRE ME' on it, or the entrepreneur outside a train station handing out flyers of her floristry business to local commuters with a beat the January blues discount code. This might sound like a lot more effort than you're used to, but if you're only following the traditional ways of putting yourself out there, you could get lost in the shuffle and feel drained from getting the same results. This chapter is all about stepping into the new version of yourself, so be open to trying new approaches – it might actually be the thing that fast tracks you to the front of the queue.

Get your taxi pitch ready

I know, the idea of an elevator pitch can make people cringe, especially for us Brits who don't even use the word 'elevator'. The last thing we want to do is start pitching ourselves in a lift – we prefer an awkward silence, looking at the floor and avoiding eye contact, right? But as someone who's pitched more than a few ideas in my time, I can tell you it's really important to have something ready for those unexpected moments. So, forget the elevator pitch, let's go for something more relatable: your **taxi pitch**. What do I mean by this? Well, one night after hosting an event, I jumped in a black cab and had an unforgettable conversation with the driver:

> **Driver:** 'What have you been doing this evening?'
> **Me:** 'I've been speaking at an event.'
> **Driver:** 'What was it about?'
> **Me:** 'I run a business called F*ck Being Humble. It was about believing in yourself and being more confident.'
> **Driver:** 'F*ck Being What?!'

Me: 'F*ck Being Humble. I help people claim what they deserve in their career and take up more space. I wrote a book on the topic.'
Driver: 'Is it on Amazon?'
Me: 'Yep, next day delivery.'
Driver: 'I'm buying it right now, I need that . . . ordered.'

In less than six minutes I had managed to convert my driver, someone who might not fit my usual target audience, into a new paying customer, and I did it without him having any prior knowledge of me or my expertise. I did it in three concise steps:

Step One: I created intrigue by telling him I'd spoken at event and my business was called F*ck Being Humble. I can guarantee no one will have said those three words to him that night.
Step Two: I explained HOW I help people by describing a common desire many people want to aspire to reach: feeling valued and being noticed.
Step Three: I mentioned a sellable product, my book. A book can often signal to others that you are a voice of authority and it's an entry-level price that many people can access easily.

Even after a fourteen-hour day, I didn't fumble my words, get awkward or shut the conversation down, because I've spent many years having conversations with strangers and getting comfortable with sharing my story. You never know who and where you might meet someone who could become a supporter or open doors for you. In an article for London Business School, psychologist Thomas Mussweiler explained: 'Research has shown that first impressions predict the way we continue to think or feel about a person over time. In other words, that initial feeling or inference about someone tends to stick – almost no matter what. Even if they're off base or partly inaccurate, first impressions really do matter because of the way they shape our ongoing perceptions.'[6] Let's look at how you could take my taxi pitch example and apply it to your situation:

> **In a networking situation**
>
> **Stranger:** What brought you here tonight?
> **You:** I recently switched careers from IT to floristry and I'm really keen to connect with more like-minded business owners doing their own thing.
> **Stranger:** That's amazing, what made you move into floristry?
> **You:** I loved gifting flowers to my friends and, when I realised it brought as much joy to them as it did to me, I decided I wanted to pursue it as a career, as a way of spreading more happiness into people's lives, especially in a forever gloomy world.
> **Stranger:** That's so true, whenever I get flowers it makes my day.
> **You:** If you're open to it, I'd love to take your details and send you a free bouquet?
> **Stranger:** That's so kind of you, thank you, sure, here's my business card. Thanks so much!
>
> **At a family occasion:**
>
> **Family member:** How's work going?
> **You:** It's going well, thanks. I've actually decided to switch careers, I'm starting a new job as a midwife next month.

> **Family member:** That's quite the move, what experience have you got to do that?
>
> **You:** Well, I've been attending a part-time course on midwifery, I have four kids of my own and in my old job I worked in a lot of fast-paced, high-pressure environments. So I'm excited to take on the next challenge, it feels like the right next step, and I love the idea of helping bring new life into the world.
>
> **Family member:** You should chat with your cousin Andrew. I think his wife made a career change into something more meaningful and really enjoyed it.
>
> **You:** That's a great idea, I'd love to talk to someone who's been through something similar. It's always helpful to hear other people's stories.

Put your eggs in multiple baskets

One of the biggest mistakes we can make in our careers is limiting ourselves to just one option. Sure, you might be leaving your job to chase your dream of working for [insert company name], but more options are always better than putting all your eggs in one basket. If you're diving into a new industry, you might need to take a few steps to work your way up or build more experience before landing that dream role or getting into a top-tier company. So, instead of getting discouraged if things don't go exactly as planned, I want you to be strategic about your next move. For example, if you're aiming to land a spot at Nike's football department, think about all the other companies or industries that you could work for instead:

Dream: Job At Nike

Copa90: A digital platform dedicated to football culture, Copa90 offers roles related to media, marketing, and content creation for football fans around the world.

The FA (Football Association): Working for a governing body like The FA could give you a behind-the-scenes look at the structure of English football, from grassroots to elite competition.

Football Clubs: Working with football clubs and their commercial and marketing departments offers opportunities to work in football branding, merchandise, community engagement and digital strategy.

Soccershop/Kitbag: Specialising in football merchandise, including jerseys, equipment and fan gear, this is a smaller but solid company to get your foot in the door.

Fan Engagement and Media Agencies: Companies that focus on fan engagement, digital content and social media marketing in football. Think about working in influencer partnerships or creating football-related content for brands.

Soccermetrics (Data Analytics): With the rise of data-driven decision-making in sports, companies like

> Soccermetrics provide advanced analytics services for football clubs, brands and agencies.
>
> **Large-scale Sporting Events:** Working for races like The London Marathon in a PR, operations or community engagement role.

You might find unexpected opportunities and connections that get you closer to where you want to be. Keep your options open and stay focused on the bigger picture!

Don't wait to be invited, invite yourself

If there's one piece of advice I could tattoo on my body (you know, if I was into motivational quote tattoos and didn't have such a low pain threshold), it would be: 'Don't wait to be invited, invite yourself.' I'm sure you can think of someone in your life who has this outlook. They're the ones who don't waste their time jumping through hoops to please others or wait for someone to give them the green light. They take matters into their own hands, carve out their own space and make things happen. I want you to do the same. If you have a goal, a dream or an ambition, don't sit around waiting for someone else to tell you it's your turn. This mantra has been the heart and soul of my brand and the permission slip I needed to go after everything I've ever wanted. Whether it was asking for opportunities, putting myself out there or simply speaking up when others wouldn't, the moments where I acted without waiting for permission have been some of my proudest. These include:

- When I wanted to become a public speaker. I didn't wait until I was invited by the industry, I hosted my own event and booked myself as the lead act.
- When I wanted to make the Forbes Under 30 List. I didn't wait for someone in my industry to recognise my contributions, I nominated myself and made the list for Europe at 28.
- When I wanted to build the awareness of my business in New York. I didn't wait before I grew a US audience to prove my resonance, I negotiated a speaking slot in New York as part of my contract and the movement grew from there.

It's easy to convince yourself that you haven't 'earned' the right to be bold, especially when you're making a career twist or shifting directions. You might think you need more experience, more qualifications or more time before you can fully own your new path, but this is where knowing your worth comes in. If you want great opportunities to come to you, you need to put yourself on the map in the first place. Waiting for a seat at the table might take longer than you think, so my advice is to make your own table and be the host.

Interview Spotlight

I interviewed Joe Thompson who twisted from working in corporate video production to a role as a probation officer in the civil service.

What made you want to change into this new industry? Was there a specific moment?

It wasn't a long-held ambition. I studied sociology at university and, though I remember being interested in criminology, wasn't encouraged to follow that path. I'd always wanted to be a documentary maker because I'd always been fascinated by people, their stories and their motivations. At the company where I was doing corporate video production, however, I became aware that we were only ever a few bad months away from me losing my job. My partner and I wanted to buy a house, so I really wanted to find something with more stability and a better trajectory. After doing some research about probation, I mentioned it to a friend who happened to give me the number of someone who had experience in that line of work. I had a chat with him, and he was just really nice and helpful. Then I did some volunteering to help gain some experience in probation work, and the people were kind – which is always a good sign. If you have an interest in something, it definitely benefits you to talk about it with friends, because you never know who can help.

How did you get the job? Was there anything that you think helped you secure the new role, given that you had limited prior experience?

I got a job that involved doing a 21-month qualification – four days a week working and one day a week studying. To get the job, I had to do a written application, an assessment day and a roleplay interview. In comparison to my old job, what I do now is behaviours and strengths based. Obviously, I have experience that does map onto that, but I'd say how you respond and handle situations is more important than anything technical. For me, people described me as calm in every job and workplace I've been in, which I think really fits with the career I was changing to. They knew I was changing careers and might not have the lived experience, so it was more about the fact I could handle the cases and had emotional resilience.

What do you wish you'd have known? How did people react to your job change?

You have to be accepting of your own preferences and know yourself. One of the reasons why I see my current career as an improvement for me over what I was doing before is because it's more in harmony with my values. My personal network is not very job-oriented – people in my family don't derive their value from work, so I don't consider my job to be an entire reflection of who I am as a person but, at the same time, I'm glad it fits who I am more closely. My close friends knew that I wasn't that happy towards the end of my last job, and so they were just pleased for me that I was doing something new.

Is there anything before changing careers you wish you'd have done?

I was in my early thirties when I changed careers. We did have some savings, but I still made sure I maintained my existing job until I had the new offer to minimise any financial risk. Being paid to work and study was a massive enabler for me being able to switch careers – it's definitely important to get yourself in the healthiest financial position, whether that means you need to live at home for a couple of years or change your spending habits. You absolutely need a plan, and it shouldn't be an impulsive and emotional decision.

From a financial perspective, what has your journey been like?

I did take a pay cut initially – it's actually the second time I've done that in my career. Job security was more important to me than a higher salary, given the long-term goals we had. Now I'm qualified and have a couple of years of experience under my belt, I'm comfortably earning more than I was before, and have a better earning potential too. I also feel really supported with my progression. I recently received a really clear and informative training session about how to get promoted to the next level/become a manager. I know exactly how much the pay goes up in each grade and it feels great to have that transparency – in my old job, you had to secure a big contract and then pitch yourself to your boss about why you deserve to have a pay rise or promotion. More entrepreneurial people might prefer it this way, but that doesn't suit my character.

Do you think this is your forever career or are you open to changing?

It could be either. The varied nature of the civil service means that there are many different jobs, routes and

> development paths I can go down. There's also lots of professions I can explore within probation; I don't have to just manage cases; I could do the training, teach people, work in the courts, work in a prison, or even specialise in the national security division like a friend of mine has. So yes, it's likely I'll stay in this career for a while, but I would also never say never to trying something new. I'm what they call a second careerist. I've already had one career in a totally different sector, so would I do the same thing if I felt bored and unfulfilled? Yes, I definitely would.

Twist – Final Thoughts

Now that we've reached the end of the chapter, I want to leave you with this: making a career twist is a rollercoaster ride with many ups and downs. There will be some moments when you question your sanity and your choices, but ultimately, it could also be the adventure that lights you up for the next ten, twenty or even thirty years of your working life. As we've discussed, it's not just about taking the leap, it's about careful planning, being okay with being a beginner again and getting really strategic about how you position yourself through self-promotion. Whether you're leaving behind a career you've known for years or simply moving into a new industry, having a solid exit strategy is key, so take a step back and really reflect on what you've gained in your current role, what you need for your next step, and how you can bridge that gap.

When you're used to being an expert in your field, change is daunting. But embracing this phase with openness and curiosity will allow you to learn faster, build resilience and gain a sense of mastery over time. Remember, no one starts as a pro, and success doesn't just fall into anyone's lap. Career twists require proactivity, persistence and grit. Keep pushing forward, even when it feels like things aren't moving fast enough.

CHAPTER 5
TAP OUT
WHAT TO DO WHEN YOU WANT TO DECENTRE WORK

When I told people I was writing a chapter on 'tapping out' I was met with looks of intrigue, excitement and relief. So far in this book we've explored how to reignite that career spark and follow a career path that is more aligned to you personally, but what we haven't explored yet is how to decentre work. For clarity the phrase 'tap out' in this book means to 'tap out of work being your identity'. It is not 'quiet quitting' or doing nothing for the rest of your life – it is focusing on who you are if you choose for work to not define you.

Now, more than ever, people are realising that devoting their existence to their job hasn't been serving them (and will continue not to do so). People are waking up to the fact that they can give their entire life to their career and be laid off in an instant, or they can spend years building a business only to realise they've missed out on core memories with their children that they'll never be able to recreate. They've observed that in most environments the harder you work and the higher up you get, the more you are met with more stress, pressure and unhappiness. So much so that younger generations in corporate companies are reportedly opting out of striving for middle management and leadership roles because they don't believe it's worth the payout. Aaron Flarin, a Gen-Z employee, shared online that rather than climbing the corporate career ladder he was instead choosing to descend it, with the hope that he stopped dreaming about his job. He explained: 'I don't want to get promoted, make more money and then spend that money on more therapy and food because I'm stressed about my job. The only wheel I want to reinvent is "work hard, play hard", how about "work medium, play medium"?'[1.]

This awakening has sparked online trends such as the 'Lazy Girl Era', where people are intentionally seeking out low-stress jobs they know won't drain them, and 'Soft Life Living', where they make downtime sacred and practise saying no to things that zap energy to create a slower pace for their life. I've observed people in their twenties taking career breaks so they can learn how to separate their work from their life and to stop tying their self-worth to their paycheque. These trends are spearheaded by newer generations who are redefining what ambition looks like. They're vocal about rejecting the career paths that millennials and boomers once followed, choosing instead to carve their own routes.

But it's not just Gen-Z challenging the work-obsessed culture, millennials are starting to see that following in the boomer footsteps hasn't actually teed them up to reach those life milestones they thought they would. Every generation feels exhausted from going above and beyond, only to realise that we are setting ourselves up to live unsustainable and unbalanced lives with zero energy to explore who we are when our career doesn't take centre stage.

In this chapter we're going to explore how you can disconnect from your career being your identity. We will explore how to identify who you are without work, how to make changes to enjoy your life more, and how to ignore external influences in order to sustain this outlook on life.

Who Am I Without Work? – Breaking Up With Your Career

I'll be honest, when I came to writing this chapter, I knew I was going to find it difficult. Not because I didn't believe it was important, but because I struggled to imagine tapping out myself. Like many people who feel they've 'found their calling', the thought of stepping back or detaching myself from my career felt counterintuitive. Why would I tap out of work being my identity when I'm really proud of the work identity I have created? Surely, the fact that I've found my dream career and I'm living it is the goal? But as I journeyed through my many interviews and discussions with people who are proactively choosing to tap out, it dawned on me that I don't know who I am when I take my career out of the story.

This feeling wasn't a new one either. I remember the strange, early days of the pandemic so clearly: as a restaurant-loving, cinema-going, cocktails-on-a-Friday-night-surrounded-by-friends kind of girl, I, along with everyone else, suddenly found my hobbies outside of work to be unavailable to me. With limited resources to keep us entertained, our interests became our new form of peacocking . . . which for me was quite painful. Every day we saw the banana-bread bakers proudly posting their latest loafs on social media, exercise enthusiasts working out wherever they could find five metres of distance outside and, quite literally, everyone (and I mean everyone) starting a podcast. At this point, I remember having a semi-mild panic attack that I had zero hobbies – it felt like I was watching a continuous talent show that I couldn't participate in. I didn't want to skip, cooking was not a calming experience in the kitchen (my fiancé can confirm) and the group Zoom quizzes were soul-destroying. So, during this period of time when I could have been exploring my personal identity and life outside of work, I decided to do what I knew I was good at – throw myself into my career. I worked ridiculously long hours, was glued to my phone and chased any career success I could find. As a small business owner, I would argue that I was doing anything to help my business survive, but when I reflect back now, I think I was actually doing anything to avoid figuring out who I really am when I don't have my armour of work on.

Fast forward to the present five years later, and it's only just now that I'm delving into who I am without work. The truth is, for many of us, throwing ourselves into our work identity is easier than figuring out what our personal identity is. With careers, there are often progress plans in place, hoops to jump through, etiquette to follow and trajectories to work towards. But with our personal identities, we are responsible for defining what this looks like and with that comes a sense of fear and vulnerability. Being able to embrace your identity without your job requires you to express your real self, which, if we're honest with ourselves, we're not always great at. Humans have a herd mentality: we follow the norms and do everything we can to fit in. When you live in a capitalist society that puts workaholism on a pedestal, the very notion of expressing yourself outside of work can seem abstract, especially if your extra-curricular hobbies don't align with the identity you've created in your career or your existing social circles.

What I've realised whilst writing this book is just how conditioned we have become to believing that our careers are the answer to our identity. From the age of five we are asked: 'What do you want to be when you grow up?' and in almost every new adult interaction, the first question asked after you've shared your name is 'What do you do?' The question is an easy ice-breaker because we assume that the majority of people we speak to work, but the question can also create a sense of judgement. In the UK especially, it can often be used as a way to measure someone's status, popularity and contributions to society, which further drives people to work harder so they can pass the test of social approval.

Therefore, before we can detach from work being our identity, I think it's important for us to explore why we are so dependent on our careers.

Being addicted to work numbs the pain

I know what you're thinking, labelling your current relationship to work as an addiction is extreme. But if you knew someone who dedicated all their energy to something that was making them withdraw from other facets of life, wouldn't you call it an addiction? The problem with our understanding of addiction is that we assume it has to be visibly destructive or socially unacceptable for us to take it seriously. If you turned up to work drunk, you'd most likely get sacked, but if you prided yourself on working excessive hours you'd probably get promoted. Workaholism is a socially validated addiction and often one that you don't think warrants an intervention. It's not like you're in hospital from drink driving or you've gambled away your possessions, so it can't be that serious, right? With a work addiction, your warning signs can easily be dismissed. Like when you're working long hours, even when it's not needed, it's fine because that's 'just the way you are'. Or when you're losing sleep over projects not being completed, it's fine because it's just a 'busy period'. Or when you're having extreme emotional reactions to things going wrong, it's fine because you just 'care about your work' so much. Except it's often not fine. Whether you realise it or not, your tendency to think about work non-stop adversely affects other aspects of your life. You've become so used to this pace of working that it's become the norm.

Now I want to be clear, a work addiction is not defined by the number of hours you put in, but by the relationship you have with work. The Bergen Work Addiction Scale was created to measure work addiction where individuals rate statements with a scale of never, rarely, sometimes, often and always. Some of the statements you might be asked during an assessment include:

- You think of how you can free up more time to work.
- You work in order to reduce guilt, helplessness, depression and anxiety.
- You've been told to reduce your time working but ignore those requests.
- You spend much more time working than you initially intend.
- You become stressed when you are not able to work.
- You lower the importance of hobbies, fun activities and fitness in exchange for more work time.
- You work so much that it has negatively impacted your health.

Research related to the scale published in the *Scandinavian Journal of Psychology* indicates that if you can answer 'often' or 'always' to at least four of these items, you may have a work addiction.

The problem today, however, is that because we have, as a society, collectively normalised overworking, it's becoming increasingly difficult to detect whether we do in fact have unhealthy relationships with our careers. When I spoke to some of my friends who love what they do about this subject, many of them were tentative to label their relationship to work an addiction. One friend said, 'I mean, I do spend every single minute of the day thinking about my business, but I don't think I'm a work addict.' People were mildly defensive when confronted with the idea and were definitely in no rush to make changes.

Speaking to career coaches on this topic, many shared that part of the reason we have an addiction to work is because we're avoiding addressing painful feelings, experiences or problems outside of work. Wendy O'Beirne, a life coach who works with high-achieving professionals, explained that 'Work lets you soothe your emotions whilst also letting you bypass them, too. If you're highly productive at work, it soothes your emotions because you feel valuable. If you feel good at work that makes it a safe place to be, and then work becomes a distraction for the things we might want to avoid outside of it.' As Wendy shared this insight with me, I couldn't help but think of all the times in my life where I had chosen to throw myself into work because it was easier than dealing with what I was going through personally. Over the last twelve months in particular, I have overcommitted, overworked and overlooked my need to deal with a traumatic event because I preferred being the 'work version' of me than the lesser capable or weaker version of me that needed to recover. Achieving a high from working helped to suppress emotions that felt too big to unbox. It was much more comfortable to have those in my circle praise me for 'smashing it right now' than it was for them to see that underneath I was deeply struggling. As I've been writing this book, I've found it both fascinating and confronting that even during the most difficult time of my life I've continued to put my career above everything, despite it contributing negatively to my wellbeing.

And then the flip side is we feel a sense of shame to even be speaking about our obsession with work with anything other than gratitude and recognising our privilege. We asked for this life or pursued this career journey, so we should learn to get on with it, power through and suck it up. Parents or grandparents will likely tell you that back in their day they had to do more with less, and in much less hospitable environments – which is absolutely true, there's no denying that. But they also had their working hours signalled to them by how much daylight there was to complete their outdoor labour, or they had unions that championed putting workers first. They had the benefit of switching off because hyper-addictive technology wasn't present in their working days and especially not after hours. The reality is two things can co-exist. In her book, *Unbending Gender*, law professor Joan Williams describes the workplace as having been built around 'ideal workers': someone who is efficient, logical, non-emotional, hard-working and available all the time, without personal commitments. The ideal worker is also expected to travel and relocate as necessary, start in their early twenties and work right up until retirement with no breaks.[2] The problem with this ideal is that it is based on an outdated family model that depends upon someone being able to look after the household full time. That is so far from reality now and yet it's still the defining principle which shapes our working lives.

And for the parents that I spoke to, there's another layer. Many reported feeling the pressure to make going back to work 'worth it' after having children, in an attempt to justify precious time away from their families. They found that securing promotions, pay rises and bigger contracts became more important to them, as if becoming more valuable in the workplace could lessen the sacrifice of not being able to spend time with their children. Ironically, obtaining these things required them to work longer hours and devote even more of their energy to their jobs.

There are so many factors that apply to why we could be addicted to work and what keeps us addicted, but the thing that kept popping up in all of my interviews was 'avoidance'. We overwork to avoid what might be too difficult to address, and if we want to change how we interact with work we might first need to sit in the discomfort of feeling the emotions we have been distancing ourselves from.

Signs you might be addicted to work:

- **Constantly thinking about work, even when not working**. You find it difficult to disengage from work, even during your downtime. Your mind is constantly preoccupied with tasks, emails, deadlines or ideas related to your job, even when you're off the clock.
- **Neglecting personal relationships**. Your relationships with family, friends or partners are suffering because of your work commitments. You may cancel plans or miss important events, and those close to you feel neglected or unimportant.
- **Difficulty saying no to extra work**. You often over-commit to projects, tasks or responsibilities, even when you're already stretched thin. You feel compelled to take on more work, even if it negatively affects your well-being or work-life balance.
- **Overworking despite negative consequences**. Even when your work habits lead to negative consequences, like health issues, damaged relationships or a decline in job performance, you keep working excessively without taking action to change.
- **Work is your primary source of self-worth**. Your identity and self-esteem are closely tied to your work and professional achievements. If you're not working or achieving success at work, you feel lost or inadequate.

CAREER COMEDOWN

Hyper-independence is all you can rely on

As a millennial obsessed with R&B, I used to proudly belt out the lyrics to Destiny's Child's *Independent Women* – 'The watch on my wrist, I bought it. The house I live in, I bought it, the car I'm driving, I bought it, because I depend on me.' It was a song that empowered millions of women around the world to depend on themselves and no one else. But what happens when our independent lifestyle is only possible if we are working excessively?

If you're a self-starting fiercely independent person, you'll likely be able to make decisions alone, generate your own motivation and consider yourself to be a responsible candidate in the working world. But whilst all these attributes might have been celebrated in your career to date, I want you to think about how your hyper-independent mindset might be contributing to your unhealthy relationship with work. If you're unfamiliar with the term, hyper-independence refers to an individual's attempts to be fully independent in all things, even when it is not helpful or when they genuinely need help or support from others. This can often be a response to a past trauma, such as neglect, and can lead to challenges in relationships and emotional connections. The reason you're addicted to work might be because at some point in your life you were forced to fend for yourself and the thing that enabled you to stand on your own two feet was your job. Maybe you left home at an early age, didn't have a family to fall back on if things went wrong or experienced something that led to you feeling isolated. If so, it's possible that throwing yourself into work was not only a good distraction but a necessity to survive.

It's not uncommon for hyper-independent people to be the older sibling or feel like the forgotten child in the family. Older siblings can often take on more care duties at a younger age or can be expected to find out the answers alone, whilst the forgotten child is used to other people taking up all the space, time or love, and has no choice but to separate themselves from the noise. When you are hyper-independent, you are likely to put on everyone else's oxygen mask before putting on your own. Your external hard armour means people come to you for support because they want to be more self-sufficient, more resilient, more capable of figuring things out alone, and you help because you want to live up to your hyper-independent reputation. Over the years you've probably said things like, 'I have no other option but to work' or, 'If I don't do it, it won't get done' – statements that might be true but kept you isolated and needing to devote your life to work. Making work your priority has moved you forward in life, so to slow down or change the way you work could risk you losing your self-built stability.

A 2019 study published in *Frontiers in Psychology* suggests that people who define themselves largely by their work are at a higher risk of developing work addiction. Since hyper-independent individuals often hold themselves to high standards and are used to doing everything by themselves, they may feel they can't afford to stop working or 'fail' in any aspect of their career.[3] Your disconnection with the external world means many of your relationships are surface level so you don't have people to bring you outside your own world. And even when you do see glimmers of hope in new relationships or interests, the minute it seems like they're taking you away from your career, you retreat because nothing is worth risking what you've spent so long building.

You might also fit into the category of people who claim only you can do your job or run your business, so you reject any suggestions of outsourcing or delegating. If you're reading this and identifying with any of the above, I want you to be thinking about what it is you really need in your life right now and in the years to come. What would it look and feel like to put on your oxygen mask first, or to even let someone else do it for you? I know it might be scary to walk away from this way of living, but just because it's all you've ever known, or it was the card you were dealt, doesn't mean you can't open yourself up to existing in this world differently.

Signs you might be hyper-independent:

- **You avoid asking for help, even when you're overwhelmed.** You'd rather struggle through a task on your own than ask for help, even when your plate is overflowing. You tend to think that asking for assistance is a sign of weakness, or that no one else can do the job as well as you can.
- **You take on more than you can handle.** You regularly say 'yes' to additional projects, assignments or responsibilities even when you're already stretched thin. You don't delegate tasks to others and prefer to take them on yourself because you feel like you're the only one who can handle them properly.
- **You avoid teamwork or group projects.** Whilst you're happy to collaborate on a surface level, you prefer working solo. You feel uncomfortable when you're required to rely on the efforts or ideas of others, and you often take on more than your fair share in group settings just to keep things moving.
- **You can't let go of perfectionism.** You set impossibly high standards for yourself and others. You feel that if you don't do something perfectly, you're failing. As a result, you often take on more work to avoid delegating tasks or admitting that something could be imperfect.

- **You overwork and have difficulty setting boundaries.** You're always the first one in and the last one out of the office, even if it's not necessary. You struggle to set healthy work-life boundaries and often work late into the night or on weekends because you feel compelled to keep going on your own.
- **You feel like asking for feedback is a threat to your independence.** When it comes to feedback or performance reviews, you may feel that receiving constructive criticism or advice from others is a personal attack, as if it's an infringement on your autonomy. You'd rather figure things out on your own, even at the cost of not improving as quickly.

Hyper-productivity means you're never left behind

Are you busy all the time? Never feel like you've got enough time to fit everything in? Worried if you don't do that extra thing you'll miss out? If so, you're most likely functioning from fear that if you're not always productive, you're going to be left behind. I can speak confidently on this subject area, because I live in this mindset all too often. I'm sure we can all think of people in our lives whose personal brand is based on one thing – being busy. They rush from meeting to meeting because they are so busy, skip lunch because they are so busy, and they can't make social plans because they are so busy. But have you ever questioned why these people insist on being so busy?

Now, I won't deny that there are many businesses that overload employees with too much work, but what I want to zoom in on in this section is all the times where you've allowed yourself to become more busy, even when you didn't need to. When have you overcommitted or signed up to taking on more when you were already at capacity? What led you to saying yes instead of saying no? For me, I'd convinced myself that if I'm busy, I have value. The most obvious times this has crept up for me was when I attempted to rest. Unless I was on a beach holiday and I'd mentally prepared to physically rest, I've always felt the need to be productive with my time. If I'm going for a walk, I have to listen to a personal development podcast; if I'm sitting watching a film after work, I have to be sending emails at the same time; if I'm on the train on the way to a meeting, I need to be brainstorming social content. And it wasn't just my professional life that had to be 100mph, it was my outside of work plans too. My exercise routine was never simply to move and enjoy being in my body – it had to be an hour of intense cardio until I felt I could no longer push myself further every single time. I could never turn down opportunities because I was convinced that every request, invite or engagement could transform my company. And if I didn't have plans on the weekend my laptop would be open and I'd be chipping away at my never-ending to-do list. My brain couldn't switch off even when I'd pay for self-care moments like massages – instead of tuning out to the sounds of raindrops and pianos, I'd be brainstorming my next big idea.

It wasn't until I recorded a podcast episode with two friends titled *That Feeling When You Have to Rest* that I realised how bad I was at just existing. In the run-up to the recording, I vividly remember overworking and staying up later than I needed to research the topic of rest, so I had something of value to say on the podcast (which of course highlighted my addiction to overworking and was completely counterintuitive to the theme of the show).

Whilst researching the topic, I discovered that there are seven types of rest that we all need in life which are:

1. **Physical:** Rest that involves your body, such as sleep, exercise, yoga or stretching.
2. **Mental:** Rest that gives your brain a break from thinking and focusing too hard.
3. **Sensory:** Rest that involves unplugging from external stimuli and giving your senses a break.
4. **Emotional:** Rest that involves processing emotions and feeling like you can share them with others.
5. **Social:** Rest that involves spending time with friends and family who bring out the best in you.
6. **Creative:** Rest that involves activities that help you feel inspired, such as listening to music, being around nature, or pursuing a creative hobby.
7. **Spiritual:** Rest that involves activities that provide meaning, such as volunteering, spiritual practice or community involvement.

This might not be news to some of you reading this book, but it was the first time I realised that resting was not just a physical state of lying down and binge-watching my favourite Netflix show on a hangover day.

During my podcast preparation, I also realised that my hyper-productive work style had originated from my business starting as a side hustle. When I first launched my company, I was working full time in a highly demanding job, so the only time I could give to growing my vision was before 9am, during my lunch break and the afterhours until I went to bed. This boundary-less style of work had created a norm of hyper-productivity and an always-on mindset that continued long after I quit nine to five and took on my side hustle as a full-time role. The scary realisation I now had was that the only person insisting I worked at this hyper-productive rate was me. I couldn't blame it on a demanding boss or a CEO who just piled on work. I had become so accustomed to this working style that it was my baseline, and I didn't see anything wrong with it. Every time I checked one app, I closed it and went to the next, seeking updates that weren't there.

With all this in mind, the thing I want you to really reflect on is how can you be *non-productive*? Yes, you read that right. Can you go for a walk without checking your step count has hit 10k or listening to self-improvement podcasts? Can you go to a spa day without sharing a robe selfie to update everyone that you're having some R & R? Can you tick off some of those hobbies you've been wanting to try without documenting it as a 'Stepping-out-of-my-comfort-zone' TikTok series? Being non-productive is doing things for joy even when they don't improve us; it's being curious and experimenting; it's opening conversations; it's just existing in the present moment. It's something we all need but something we rarely do. I can't say I've nailed this fully but, whilst writing this book and having these revelations, I have been trying to implement what I'm sharing and I'm honestly noticing a dramatic improvement in my enjoyment of life.

Signs you're hyper-productive:

- **You feel rest is a waste of time.** When you do take a break or rest, you feel a deep sense of guilt, as though you're wasting time that could be used more productively. You struggle to justify taking time for yourself, even when you're exhausted.

- **You believe being busy equals success.** You equate being constantly busy with being successful or productive. The more you work, the more you feel accomplished, even if your work quality or your mental and physical health are suffering as a result.
- **You've lost touch with personal hobbies or interests.** Your hobbies, interests, or passions outside of work have taken a backseat because you've prioritised tasks that are career related. You no longer remember what it's like to engage in something purely for enjoyment or personal fulfilment.
- **Everything you do needs to be measured.** Any extra-curricular activities you do have to be quantified to prove that your time is worth investing. You dislike doing activities that you're not seeing quick results or growth from.
- **Prioritising performing over self-care.** Self-care practices such as eating properly, exercising or relaxing are pushed aside to make more time for self-improving. You sacrifice your health and well-being in favour of getting more done.

Over-achieving proves your worth

One of the hardest things I've had to reckon with in my career is that overachieving to prove your worth is not a long-term or sustainable plan and it doesn't actually make you happy. You might think that overdelivering or outdoing other people is what will lead to more people valuing you, but actually all you end up with is exhaustion and disappointment. The arrival fallacy is the outlook that when you reach your goal everything is going to be great, but the truth is life has to be lived in the middle and the middle is the present moment. If you're always deferring joy for when you achieve something or striving to prove the doubters wrong, all you're ever focusing on is external validation.

The question that has popped up a lot whilst writing this book has been: 'When is enough, enough?' You might think that you'll be satisfied when you get that director title, or that you'll have made it when you get that company car, but I am sharing from experience that that moment is always more anti-climactic than you think, especially if you're chasing it to prove yourself to other people.

Throughout my life, I never felt celebrated for being smart. It was something that I felt everyone else around me was, but I gravitated towards more creative activities and, as a result, I always felt people didn't always take me that seriously. Despite getting promotions and pay rises every year, running a successful international business, writing a book and changing people's lives for the better, I still felt judged in the same way by the same people. It took a while for me to realise that killing yourself at work just to get people's approval is never worth the wait, and it's even more deflating to realise that some people will always struggle to congratulate you. What's five seconds of praise if you've spent five years being unhappy and your trajectory looks much of the same? You might have used your ambition as the driving force to get to where you are, but if your ambitions are based around popularity, you are striving towards something that can only be defined by what others deem to be important.

Based on the interviews I conducted, overachieving is a common trait amongst individuals whose families had immigrated to a country to provide their children with the best possible opportunities. A pressure to not just do well but to be the best in the class because they are likely to face differential treatment leads to many children of immigrant families striving to overachieve. As well as the internal pressure they place on themselves, they also must contend with passed down family expectations and generational sacrifices.

When I spoke to Mardin Nari, whose family, originally from Iraq, immigrated to the UK, she told me, 'All I saw growing up was my dad working so hard, he was constantly in survival mode. Seeing him do that put a lot of pressure on me. As a result, I've often felt the need to prove myself as an immigrant and make use of everything I have available. He didn't have access to the education I did, so I had to go to university, get the best grades and all to secure a reputable job.' For others overachieving stems from childhood wounds of parents separating or being absent in formative years, having to live up to narratives that were formed and created before you were even born, or being part of a family where overachieving is engrained in their DNA; if you want to represent the family name you too should follow in the same footsteps.

From all of my research and observations, the common underlying needs overachievers are searching for are belonging, acceptance and validation. You might have even said, 'When I do _____ I'll be able to prove to them I'm worth it' or 'I just need to do _____ and they will take me seriously'. What's important to observe in these statements is that they centre someone else's feelings over your own. In case you need reminding, your value is not based on the output you generate.

Mel Robbins, motivational speaker and podcaster, explored the topic of self-worth and business on her podcast when she interviewed trauma expert, psychologist and medical doctor, Dr Scott Lyons.[4] He encouraged listeners to reflect on: 'How if, at all, did you feel loved as children? How did we understand our value or worth? Was it freely given to us, or did we have to do something in order to get something?' Most of the times we have been celebrated in our childhood and adult years are linked back to something we did. Winning competitions, getting good feedback, receiving high grades. These are all things you might have received positive attention for growing up and now still, as adults, connect your self-worth to. The need for external validation keeps us performing at an unattainable rate until our bodies make the decision of no more. I know far too many people who ended up severely burning out with physical and mental side effects because their perfectionist striving became all consuming.

Signs you're an overachiever:

- **You constantly set unrealistically high expectations for yourself.** You regularly set goals or standards that are almost impossible to achieve, even when you've already accomplished significant milestones. You feel frustrated or dissatisfied when you don't meet these self-imposed expectations.
- **You struggle to celebrate your successes.** Even when you accomplish something significant, you quickly move on to the next challenge without acknowledging your achievements. You don't take the time to feel proud of what you've done, always focusing on what's next instead of what you've already achieved.
- **You feel like you're never doing enough.** No matter how much work you complete, you always feel like it's not enough. You struggle to appreciate your efforts and are constantly looking for the next task or project to tackle, even when your plate is already full.
- **You sacrifice your personal life for achievement.** You prioritise work or personal goals at the expense of your

relationships, hobbies and self-care. You often miss social events, family time or downtime because you feel the need to stay focused on your achievements.
- **You judge yourself harshly for not being perfect.** You are highly critical of yourself when things don't go perfectly, focusing only on your flaws or mistakes. Any imperfection feels like a personal failure, leading you to work even harder in an attempt to 'fix' it.

Shifting Perspectives

You might have read that section and felt seen, exposed or possibly upset – I know I did. It's not every day that someone holds a mirror up to how you might be negatively contributing to your own unhealthy work habits. But here's the thing I want to highlight: the connection between work addiction, hyper-independence, hyper-productivity and overachieving often comes down to something deeper. We often use work as a distraction, a way to avoid facing parts of our past or feelings that are just too tough to deal with. It's like we let our careers be a quick fix, a cover-up for deeper personal stuff we'd rather not confront. If you're truly ready to step away from that cycle and build a healthier relationship with work, the first step is acknowledging where you are right now. Once you've done that, we can start identifying the changes that need to happen.

Now I want to spend some time helping you to break free from some of these beliefs and societal pressures that keep you stuck in work addiction. Let's explore how to shift your mindset and finally 'tap out' of that exhausting pattern.

CAREER COMEDOWN

1. Your career doesn't need to be your life's work

Have you ever met someone who said their career is 'my life's work'? I have, and if I'm honest I've definitely described what I do professionally as my 'life's work', too. But ever since I started writing this book, I've started to reflect on what that really means. The Collins dictionary definition says: 'Someone's life's work is the main activity that they have been involved in during their life, or their most important achievement.' Whilst it goes on to give the example that 'Sandra's garden was her life's work', I've not met many people in reality who don't think their life's work is connected to their career. The only reference I can think of are mothers who take pride in raising their children – and, whilst I think that's absolutely something to celebrate, I know many who have felt snubbed when voicing that motherhood is their life's work. The phrase itself sounds so profound, no wonder we all become obsessed with trying to find a career deemed 'worthy' enough to match. But what if your life's work has NOTHING to do with your career? What if it's instead the things that people will remember you for when you're gone?

As I write this, I'm thinking about my stepdad who dedicated his entire career to working as an accountant at one company until he retired. He gave a lot to his job and enjoyed what he did, but his 'life's work' has nothing to do with an Excel spreadsheet. In fact, if you asked anyone about the impact he's had on other people's lives, I can guarantee that almost everyone who knows him would say the main activity he's been involved in his entire life is entertaining people. It's not the office version of Phil that people talk about, it's the motivating, entertaining, high energy, gives back to the community, out-of-office Phil that people adore. What I admire about his relationship with work is that being an accountant was one facet of who he was, but rarely the leading headline. He might have completed a life at work, but his life's work is so much more than his career.

As you read this, you might be questioning how our life's work can be anything but our jobs if we spend 70 per cent of our time at work. The thing I want you to come back to is that your life's work doesn't need to be defined by your time investment. You can keep your current job because it pays the bills and also explore and dedicate yourself to what's important to you outside of your career. Whether you love gardening, cooking, spending time with your family or making people laugh, your life's work and what you leave behind is so much more than what you do to make money. So now I want you to reflect on the following:

- When you look back at the end of your life, will you be content that your life's work only consisted of your career? Or do you want to have more variation in your legacy?
- Removing your career from the equation, what would you like to look back on as your biggest achievement or the thing you spent the most time on?
- Think about someone in your life you admire. What does their 'life's work' consist of and what can you take away from their story?

2. You're not losing your title

You might be thinking that defining yourself outside of work is a nice idea, but that you're not ready to give up your title – the title you've spent years, possibly even decades, securing. You might have studied for a long period of time, passed difficult exams or even delivered multiple life-saving surgeries to earn it, so to 'tap out' would mean scrapping all of that hard work. We often assume that when we change directions or choose to follow a new way of life, it means we have to shed our identity or let go of what we've achieved. But I want you to remember that it doesn't matter whether you've spent years training in law, medicine or even to be a magician, your experience in that field doesn't evaporate overnight just because you choose to distance yourself from that line of work.

Alice or 'Alice-The-Vet', as she described herself, told me she decided to change careers because, despite spending years devoting her life to veterinary medicine, her life outside of work had become non-existent. She originally loved her role as a vet but as her career grew, she found herself exhausted, having to spend her weekends recovering from intense work schedules instead of seeing her friends. She started to resent her career but didn't want to let go of the title she'd spent so hard working for. When searching for a new job, she successfully applied to work at a vet-tech start-up where she used her veterinary experience as a selling point. Now in her new role, she told me, 'When people ask me what I do now, I still say I'm a vet. I'm not an ex-vet, I'm just doing a different job. I'm still a doctor, I still have all the knowledge, I'm just registered as a non-practising vet.'

Your title doesn't just leave you because you change roles or choose to exit a specific industry. You still earned those stripes, and you're as deserving to claim the title now as you were when you were practising the role. I'm pleased to share that, since changing careers, Alice has found time to discover who the non-vet Alice is, which led to her reconnecting deeply with friends, and move to another country. She also supports other vets navigating the industry by offering financial guidance to help people who might be feeling similar pressures to her.

This conversation really struck a chord with me and got me thinking about all the other titles people don't lose just because they're not 'practising it': a parent doesn't stop being a parent when their kids move out of the family home; an author doesn't stop being an author after only writing one book; and an Olympic athlete doesn't stop being an athlete just because they stop competing professionally. I know this chapter has so far been focused on separating your identity from your work title, but I wanted to include this story as a reminder that you can still hold onto what you're proud of in your career, even if it's not representing your daily output. Ask yourself:

- What relationship do you have with your existing title?
- Why does this title hold so much importance to you?
- How can you keep it and use it as selling point for future opportunities?

3. Your patients don't 'need you'

Have you ever been caught saying the words 'my clients need me' or 'my company needs me'? I know I have. But it wasn't until I listened to a podcast with physician Gabor Maté and podcaster Dr Rangan Chatterjee, where they discussed how toxic the outlook can be, that the penny really dropped on why we need to stop saying it. Gabor Maté very clearly highlighted to the host Dr Rangan that although the medical industry can carry a lot of pressure, he recommends letting go of the idea that your patients 'need you'.[5] What they actually need is an individual with your skillset – if you got hit by a car tomorrow, they would simply find someone else to fill in. Now, I'm not a doctor, and I'm the first to remind people that most of us (especially in the creative industries) are not saving lives. In fact, the biggest thing we are saving . . . is

PDFs. But I do want you to think about how many times you've insisted your clients, boss, colleagues and company all need you, and how often that was actually true.

The latter part of the sentence is something I've often chimed to friends and partners when I've felt like they were overworking and needed reminding that the world won't end if they don't reply to that email after hours, but it's the first part of the sentence that we really need to remind ourselves of. As great as you are, there are other people who can fill that hole, need or service, and accepting that is so important if you want to rewire your relationship to work.

Gabor went on to explain that the reason we insist that our patients need us is because we actually need our patients. Humans want to feel valued, and work fills that void well. However, when we live by the mindset of being needed, we can often end up working longer hours without taking sufficient breaks or holiday allowances, which in turn eventually erodes our ability to service others and do our job well in the first place.

- What might you be avoiding when you prioritise your work above everything else?
- When did you previously not feel needed? How did it make you feel?
- How might needing to feel needed be negatively affecting your personal life?

Giving 110 per cent is not an aspiration

If you're a hard-working overachiever, you are likely to take pride in being someone who always gives a 110 per cent in their career. You'll have probably used it as a badge of honour or unique selling point in interviews, pitches or on your CV. Or if you're like me, you might have even used it as an answer to what your weakness is at work: 'I always give 110 per cent to my work and sometimes I struggle to step away from it.' As I read that back now, I realise just how much my mind had been trained into thinking I should be proud that I gave ALL my effort to my career because it would make me more hireable. But let's explore why giving 110 per cent is silly for multiple reasons.

Firstly, it's not humanly possible to give more than 100 per cent. Imagine a glass you want to fill with water. You can only fill it 100 per cent before you end up spilling it. We'd never look at a spilt glass and consider it a cause for celebration, so why would you revere giving more than you have in your working life?

The second reason this phrase is flawed is because it leaves no room for improvement. If you are always trying to function at the maximum rate, then you'll have nothing left for key moments when more is necessary. Very few of us would sign a contract that committed us to going above and beyond every single day, though we do surprisingly allow this expectation to fester and grow in our relationships with customers and clients overtime. Although you can't always control the culture of your company, you do at some point have to take accountability for how you feed into it.

Trinh Mai, director of mindfulness programming at the University of Utah Health, advises that if people want to move away from the 110 per cent mindset, we should start by looking at where we could give 20 per cent less in selected areas that don't run the risk of harm or significant loss.[6] Doing this allows us to reckon with the reality of our humanness, rather than the illusion that we are superheroes. Trinh explains: 'Just as we cannot insist that the tomato plants in our garden produce fruit faster in the face of drought, disease or fire, we cannot demand more from ourselves than we have to give. We, too, are organisms on the planet that are compelled to cooperate with our biological design. It sounds like an underachiever to say give 80 per cent, but choosing intentionally where to reduce time and energy, working with the reality of being human, is perhaps the key to promoting quality care and sustaining ourselves.'

I also discovered an eye-opening video from Nate Daye, a straight-talking TikToker, who said the best piece of work advice he received was to make your 50 per cent your 100 per cent. He explained: 'When you get a new project and you know you can get it done in two weeks, tell them it will take four. That way when they tell you they need to speed up the timelines, you can do it in three weeks – be the hero, don't be burned out.'[7]

Granted this is not possible for every work situation, but it poses a good reminder that giving 'too much' from the outset might be why we feel like busy overworked fools. On reflection, we may actually be the ones setting the bar too high and forgetting that we have more agency than we think we do. What if before every new job, new contract or new client commitment we actively decided that the maximum percentage we would give is 70 per cent and we clearly outlined boundaries, ways of working and rules that would stop us from moving into the 110 per cent workhorse mode? If we want to have more reserves to enjoy life without work, we need to rewire our outlook that giving always 110 per cent to our careers is a good thing. We have to redistribute our efforts and start asking ourselves, How much can I sustainably give? Consider also the following:

- What are you giving too much effort to professionally?
- Where could you reduce your effort by 20 per cent? How could you start doing this?
- If you were to start from scratch, how would you split your 100 per cent capacity to different aspects of work and life?

TAP OUT

You don't need to work hard to play

We've all heard the saying 'work hard, play hard', right? It's supposed to be about balancing work and fun, putting in a shift and then rewarding yourself with some well-deserved downtime.

In the professional world, this mentality often shows up in high-pressure environments – think intense trading floors or super-competitive industries – where the more hours you put in and higher risks you take, the better an employee you look. 'Work hard, play hard' is the phrase you use for excessive spending, bad decision-making and, in many cases, doing things you might regret or that feel far from a work-life balance. But the real problem is not that we reward our hard work with playing, it's that we assume we must work hard before we can enjoy pleasures in life.

One of my friends put it perfectly: 'Why can't we just work a reasonable amount for our job and salary, and still have time to enjoy life?' It's a fair question, right? The problem is, 'work hard, play hard' is often followed by the five words 'go big or go home', which makes you feel like either you need to be putting in every ounce of effort you have to make something a success or you shouldn't try altogether. But as we've already talked about, giving that much to everything leaves us with no energy for anything else. When we refer to life in such extreme terms, we end up burning the candle at both ends. So, here's your permission slip: you don't have to earn your playtime by working yourself to the bone. You can play as hard, or as little, as you want, independent of how your work week has gone. Maybe you've had a tough couple of days and need to unwind with something fun, or maybe life just feels a bit dull and you need a pick-me-up. Play can, and should, be spontaneous. So next time you feel that pressure to earn your relaxation, I want you to let go of that. Embrace the idea that play can fit into your life at any time, on your terms.

Here are some more questions to reflect on:

- What stops you from experiencing joy?
- What habits might you have that delay you from experiencing joy?
- How can you add more play into your diary without it feeling intrinsically linked to your professional performance?

I hope as we dive into these common phrases, you're starting to get a clearer picture of where things might be going off-track in your career. But before we move forward, especially if you're a boss or business owner leading a team, I want to make something clear: tapping out doesn't mean quitting, it's about questioning the way we think work *should* be. It's about getting curious, asking ourselves why we react the way we do in certain work situations, and taking a step back to reflect on what kind of role model you want to be in your career.

Do you want to be contributing to the standard that work comes above everything no matter what? Or do you have more power and flexibility than you realise to create a different kind of environment? It's so easy to justify our actions by saying, 'I had to put work above everything to get where I am, so everyone else should too.' But that mindset isn't how real change happens. If everyone before you had slammed the door shut, you wouldn't be reaping the rewards you do now. This isn't just about creating the life you want moving forward, it's also about the legacy you can leave in your industry or for the generations to come. By making changes for yourself first, you could be part of the movement that helps reshape how we work for the better. Imagine being on the side of history, the one that helped shift the narrative. Pretty powerful, right?

What Life Do You Really Want?

So far in this chapter we've explored why we're addicted to work and the things we need to let go of if we want to live a life beyond our careers. Now it's time to reflect on the life that you want instead. In his book, *I Don't Want to Grow Up*, Scott Stillman explains that before we focus on what we need to make our dream life happen, we should start imagining what we want it to look like in the first place.[8] For example, if your goal is to travel, what does that actually look like? Where do you want to go, for how long? What do you want to do whilst you're away? Having a clear picture is the first step, as sometimes the logistics of making our dreams happen can get in the way and make us abandon them right from the start.

Now it's time for you to really think about what your dream life would look like if your career didn't lead your decision-making. I interviewed Kirsty, an HR specialist who had spent her life being a career go-getter until she got a cancer diagnosis. She was unable to work whilst undergoing treatment and told me that going through a life-altering health scare put things in a new perspective for her. 'Having cancer opens your eyes that it could all be over,' she said, before adding, 'I don't want to die having spent my life at work.' Kirsty expressed that she feels our careers have wrongly become our primary focus in life and cited Simon Squibb's video series *What's Your Dream?* as an example of how many people connect their dreams to a career-based outcome.

CAREER COMEDOWN

If you're not familiar with the series, entrepreneur and investor Simon Squibb is on a mission to help 10 million people kickstart their businesses and he searches for people to invest in by conducting street interviews asking local pedestrians 'Do you have a dream?' If you've seen these videos on your social media scrolls, you're likely to have been left feeling inspired or newly motivated. But in my interview with Kirsty she rightly highlighted that almost every person he asks says that their dream, without hesitation, is to run a business of some sort. When I asked what her dream would be if Simon Squibb were to put a microphone in front of her face, she said that she simply wants to be on a desert island with all her friends forever or living a wholesome life with her dog and husband, growing vegetables on their own plot of land.

I love Simon Squibb's approach to paying it forward with the work that he does, but this conversation got me thinking about how strange it was that instead of requesting a better quality of life from the real magic genie, people were using their one wish for a career dream to come true. Have we become so obsessed with our careers that that's all we want to wish for?

That evening I lay awake thinking about what my future would look like if my career didn't call the shots or dictate where I was. Where would I be? What would I do? Who would I be surrounded by? The next day I asked my partner. It didn't take long for him to reply to describe his ideal scenario: off grid, in a forest, making things with his hands, and eating off of natural resources. As I heard him passionately recite his answer, I laughed, relieved this wasn't one of our first date questions as we had very different dream lives. I knew that my dream life would consist of me living in a place that had consistently warmer weather, near a beach or pool and nature, somewhere that felt connected, and a place I could meet interesting people. What was crazy about this conversation with my partner was not that our fantasy lives were quite different, but that in the entire seven years of our relationship, we had never discussed what life would look like without our careers. We met in our mid-twenties and ever since we've both been focused on advancing our careers and spurring each other to achieve more professionally, without ever sparing a second to reflect on what our life could look like if we solely focused on just living instead.

Here are some questions for you to reflect on:

- What would your dream life look like if you didn't centre it around work?
- When you think of retiring, what does that look like?
- If you were to take a mini-retirement next year, what would be first on your list?
- Where would you be? What do your surroundings look like?
- Who are you with? What people do you come into contact with?
- How are you spending most of your time?
- When you're not working what are you doing?
- How much do you need to earn to sustain this life?
- What stops you from chasing after the dream life?
- Do you need to do the job you're trained in to get there? Or can you work in a different role?

Tapping Out In Real Time

So how do you actually start tapping out of your career? What if you don't want to leave your current job or working situation, but do want to find a way to reduce how much time it consumes in your mind? I've personally been testing out different approaches and have spoken to people who are in the process of tapping out in order to gather a collection of small steps to help you get started.

Let go of expectations

Earlier this year I read the book *Same as Ever: Timeless lessons on risk, opportunity and living a good life* written by Morgan Housel.[9] The book covers twenty-three short stories about the way that life, behaviour and business will always stay the same. In a world full of constant change, I found it comforting to learn that certain things do repeat themselves and that we can in fact prepare for them. In the chapter titled 'Expectations and reality – the first rule of happiness is low expectations', Housel explains that what generates emotions is the gap between expectations and reality. We spend an overwhelming amount of our time trying to get ahead, all whilst neglecting to manage our expectations about what we should get in return. As I read these words, I thought about all the times I've poured my time into work with a clear set of expectations I'd agreed in my head, but that were never signed off by the people I was working for in reality. I'm sure you know the internal dialogue:

- 'If I'm putting in all these hours, I better get that promotion.'
- 'If they don't give me a pay rise after this I'll be fuming.'
- 'I'll do this for them now, but they better do the same when I need it.'
- 'They've got to give me what I've asked for now I've done all this.'

And unsurprisingly, when those unagreed expectations weren't met in real time, I became demotivated. Having high expectations in our careers leaves many of us feeling betrayed or overlooked, but as Housel explains, if changing the circumstances is not something you're able to do with your work situation right now, the next best thing will be to change your expectations. That means moving away from the equation of 'If I do this, I should get that' and instead focusing on delivering your job in exchange for your salary and nothing more.

I spoke to Anna Reeve, who swapped her career-climbing mindset for one which prioritised her wellbeing and life beyond work. After years of feeling like she needed to be at the top of her game all the time, Anna retrained as a coach, which forced her to confront her own toxic work behaviours – from over-volunteering, to constantly performing for praise, and always needing to be the best. She explained to me, 'You can change your location and surroundings but if you're not changing how you feel about yourself and talk to yourself, then it doesn't matter where you are – you're still going to be unfulfilled'. Moving to a life-first approach meant she had to reconnect with her values, understand when her body was sending signals to slow down and embrace self- compassion. She made the decision to take a part-time role whilst she built up her coaching credentials and is intentionally finding ways to not let her part-time role become her identity. She now fulfils her role with the outlook that she can do a good job without always going far above and beyond and is extremely protective of her boundaries. She did explain to me, 'If you choose to take an intentional step back and not put yourself forward for things, you have to do so knowing and accepting that you may be overlooked for pay rises, promotions or any workplace benefits that require extra hours. If you're going to opt out of "the game", you have to be okay with the consequences and recognise that as a cycle-breaker, you'll also be the outlier'. For context, I'm not saying this is right or fair, this could actually be a red flag signal that your company or clients only reward overworkers, but I am sharing this as a reminder that changes in your input can have an impact on the output you receive.

So how do you actively let go of expectations and not let them creep back in? Well, something that has helped me is saying, 'If this is the only time this happens, I'm so proud and grateful' when amazing opportunities occur. In March 2021 I experienced my best ever financial month. I was elated and so proud of myself but, instead of enjoying the moment, I quickly became obsessed with besting that success every year. By the time the next year eventually came around, however, I was nowhere close to replicating the same number, let alone doubling it. I remember panicking that I was becoming irrelevant or assuming everyone else was doing miles better than I was, so I ended up pouring lots of hours into marketing – and only ending up with burnout and a bruised ego to show for it. The difference year on year wasn't just financial. It was also the fact that in 2022 I had gone in with high, unrealistic expectations. That experience became a grounding lesson for me as a business owner: to be grateful for when things happen but to not fixate on them needing to happen in order for me to be happy.

Now, I remind myself, 'I know what I need to survive, anything else is a bonus.' It also forced me to take note of what I did have, what else I might have gained during that period and what the cost of achieving bigger and better might have been if I'd have been successful in surpassing the previous year. It's important to note that lowering your expectations isn't about lowering your ambitions, but rather about reserving your energy for when things happen as opposed to feeling angry that they haven't.

TAP OUT

Change how you speak about work

You might not realise it, but the way you speak about work doesn't just reflect how you feel about work – it can also affect how you feel about it. If you describe every obstacle you face as a 'nightmare' or 'disaster', you are signalling to your mind and body that the problem you are being faced with requires a response similar to an emergency. When we use extreme language to describe quite common and solvable problems, we are forcing ourselves into survival mode.

I was once speaking at an event and the organiser told me they'd had an 'absolute disaster': the printers had printed their logo upside down on the balloons that would sit either side of the stage. After listening, I smiled and reminded her that this wouldn't undermine any of the hard work she'd put into planning such a great event and that it was likely no one would even notice the misprinted balloons. After the event, which was a success, we both laughed about how easy and common it is to use extreme language like this to describe things that are, by all metrics, not a big deal. Whether said for dramatic effect on a mundane day, or the result of working for someone who really does make you fearful of misprinted balloons, I need you to remember that extreme language is rarely needed at work – unless you are saving lives. A 'disaster' is a tsunami wiping out an entire village; a 'nightmare' is someone you love being hit by a car; the 'worst day of your life' might be someone you deeply care about dying. These things require that type of language – small everyday errors don't. If you want to reserve your emotional energy and capacity for other more important things in life, you need to stop speaking about speed bumps in your day as if it's the end of the world.

To help move away from speaking about work in a negative or pessimistic way, some people find it beneficial to highlight the purpose of each action on their to-do list, so they always exist in context. For example, instead of saying you're working, try reminding yourself of what the activity is:

- I'm dedicating time to my clients right now because they pay my salary.
- I'm building my business right now to help people feel more confident.
- I'm thinking of new ideas so I can attract more opportunities.

This reframe can help you feel less like you are imprisoned by work and more like you are playing, serving, experimenting or expressing yourself. On the days that you are struggling to motivate yourself, the positive reinforcements in these statements are better at mobilising you than simply telling yourself, 'I have to go to work.'

And it's not just how you speak to yourself, it's also how you receive information from others. TikToker Mary Jelkovsky stated online that to help create a distance between herself and other people's limiting beliefs she started adding 'for you' to the end of their sentences. For example, if somebody says, 'a nine to five job is the key to success' she replies in her head, 'for you'. This acts as a reminder that we have the autonomy to decide what we want for ourselves, without taking on other people's truths and opinions as default.[10] Remember, the concept of tapping out of work is going to feel so abstract to some people that they might insist it isn't possible, even if you put together a sustainable plan for yourself.

Limit your technology use

We've touched on it briefly already, but now is the time to acknowledge our addiction to technology and actively commit to changing the habits that aren't serving us. According to research from DataPortal's *Digital 2024 Global Overview Report*, the average person globally spends around six hours and forty minutes looking at a screen every day – that's a staggering 40 per cent of our waking hours.[11] Other studies have even shown that the mere presence of a smartphone, even if it's face down, distracts your brain from whatever you're doing and can reduce your ability to have a conversation, listen or engage with others.[12] So, every time you tell yourself your relationship with technology is not really distracting you from what you're doing, you're lying to yourself.

When speaking to people who have successfully 'tapped out', the majority of them stated that changing their relationship to technology was a significant factor. They make active choices, like intentionally not having their work emails on their phones so they can only check their inbox when they are online or during office hours. They let others know that they'd prefer to never use apps like WhatsApp to receive updates on work. They opt for an alarm clock for morning wake-up calls and do not use their phones within the first hour of waking up or the final hour before they go to bed.

Daisy Morris, founder of the social media consultancy The Selfhood, shared online that she had actively made the decision to delete all social media apps from her phone, despite managing her clients' profiles and her own for her work. She was struggling with overwhelm, lack of confidence, sleep and concentration, so decided to start pre-scheduling content to share in advance, blocking out time to replying to messages on her desktop when necessary, and set dedicated 'app days' twice a week to do intentional research for trends. In just one week she described the results as mind-blowing: she felt healthier, more present in conversations online and offline, more productive, and her sleep improved drastically. If Daisy, someone whose business genuinely does rely on apps and being connected, is able to put technological boundaries in place without compromising her output, then you definitely can, too.

Assess your work relationships

If there's one thing I've observed throughout my career, it's that Brits love to moan about work. According to a 2023 study conducted by Gallop, the UK's workforce is one of the most dissatisfied in Europe, with a staggering 90 per cent of UK employees lacking enthusiasm for their job.[13]

This became apparent to me every time I moved on to a new role and realised that at least half of my previous 'work besties' were besties because we bonded over frustrations in the office – something that didn't make for great chat once I'd left. In my experience, it's more socially acceptable to bitch about work than to be raving about how great it is. These relationships are great for when you need a mid-morning vent, but we need to consider that it's also possible for them to have a negative impact.

I spoke to Gen-Z employee Mardin who, after originally training as a lawyer, has started to recognise the benefits of tapping out at the age of twenty-seven. Part of that process for her is not actively pursuing work friendships outside of the office. She said that in order to keep work at work 'I'm friendly at work, I will go for lunch with colleagues, but outside of that, I don't know who you are. If you become friends with colleagues, you don't ever get to escape work. When there's a "family vibe" or "I'm your friend, can you do this for me?" it creates an imbalance.'

For some people, friendships at work are the sole thing that keep them going. For others, it drains them emotionally and adds to their mental pile when in and outside of the office. If you are the latter, I understand that it feels impossible to physically distance yourself from your colleagues without seeming rude, but here are a few things you can start to do to signal the kind of working relationship you'd like:

Slower responses to messages. If you're used to being at your work bestie's beck and call, now is the time to be actively responding more slowly to their messages and start communicating that you're trying to focus on work less after hours. By reducing how quickly you respond to them you will send a signal that you're no longer on 24/7 support.

Start taking your lunch break. If you signed a contract that includes a one-hour work break, start taking it solo out of the office. Go for walks, create space for solitude and give your mind a rest from the non-stop work discussions you might be privy to if you stay in and sit with your colleagues. Or, if you have to stay in the office, start a hobby like learning a new language or educating yourself on a new topic that requires headphones in and no distractions. Even if you're not fully invested, start using your lunch breaks as a way to separate yourself.

Focus on relationships that align to tapping out. When you do choose to hang out with people, think about how you can drive the conversation away from just moaning about work and be more curious about your colleagues out of office interests. There might be a tonne of people you've not properly connected with yet because your priority until this point has been to complain or get ahead.

Let others be the hero

Up until this point you might have been the ice-breaking, vocal, overachieving hero that saves the day or brings the energy to different work interactions. But part of the reason you might be feeling exhausted or emotionally drained at work is because you're the person that everyone can depend on to speak up first in a meeting, instigate the brainstorms or carry the conversations in networking environments. That level of consistent communication can leave you unable to show up outside of work and could be having an impact on non-work relationships. This is not me telling you to withdraw at what you're good at or stop contributing altogether, but I am encouraging you to think about what the benefits are of letting other people pick things up. Below are a few examples of how this approach could benefit you with your 'tapping out' process whilst also enabling others around you to flourish.

Benefits for you	Benefits for others
• You can manage from a distance • Meetings can take place without you needing to be present • You can concentrate on other tasks without feeling overwhelmed • You're celebrated as a leader that doesn't drown people out	• Colleagues who are quieter have more space to speak up • More collaboration and problem-solving could occur between employees • People move out of their comfort zone

It's time to stop making yourself the hero that saves every situation, and start creating space for others to step in. It's important to note that people around you might notice a change in how you're interacting – in that case, all you need to say is something like this: 'I wanted to open up space for the rest of the group to contribute before I did and ensure everyone felt they had opportunity to add value.'

Whilst we're on this topic, I want you to accept that sometimes people will put in less effort than you and it's not always your job to fix that. I'm sure you've worked with people in the past where they put in 10 per cent and you felt obliged to pick up the remaining 90 per cent to ensure the work was delivered. But if you find that this is the situation in most of your working environments, you need to be the one questioning your own involvement in the dynamic. Reaching hero status is not enjoyable if it's only ever draining you – other people need to take responsibility for themselves.

I once spoke to a high-flying CEO, who burned herself out so much, she physically lost her voice. She was still able to work, but losing her ability to speak meant she could finally listen to what was happening around her. In her case, she realised that every meeting she entered felt like a competition of updates, and when she was unable to physically input, she could finally see how little she actually cared about the topic at hand. This period of silence forced her to reflect on what she had been contributing at the company and how it no longer aligned to what was important to her. I don't want anyone reading this to get to the point of such stress and exhaustion, but the learning from this story was that sometimes our need to contribute and keep up with the work pace means we're not actually reflecting on the value of what we're offering in the first place.

CAREER COMEDOWN

Your ideas can wait

I don't know about anyone else, but when I feel like I'm running out of time to action all of the 50,000 ideas I have in mind, I attempt to do them all at once and end up burning out. Sometimes I come up with an idea that no one else has thought of and I want to beat people in the market to launching it (unhealthy mindset #1). Sometimes the empath in me hears or sees a new story that hits so deep I feel like it's my responsibility to solve it (unhealthy mindset #2). In both scenarios, I'm putting on unnecessary pressure and functioning out of fear. The fear of missing out, fear of not doing enough and fear of letting people down.

This is an ongoing problem of mine, which became glaringly obvious in the final three months of 2023. Despite already having a crammed schedule, not enough rest and low capacity, I remember going for lunch with a friend where I word-vomited a thousand new ideas at her, including a plan to pivot my business in a completely new direction, before I opened up that I was struggling outside of work too. Seeing I needed some clarity, she asked, 'What is the one thing you need to focus on until the end of the year?' The answer was obvious: it was the website rebrand I'd been banging on about for months. At the time, my business wasn't performing as well as it could have been, likely because my website had been bootstrapped and designed poorly by me five years prior. She helped me to see that although my ideas were great and timely, no one was waiting for them.

I wish I could tell you that I followed her advice explicitly. But no, obviously I still signed myself up to more than I could handle, and it took until November to realise it. By then, I had to actively start saying no to myself and to others so I could create the space I needed to concentrate. I even rebranded the month as

NO-vember as a reminder that if I wanted to enjoy my Christmas break and rest, I'd better stop overcommitting and start focusing on the priorities. The people pleaser in me struggled so much with saying no, but I realised that I don't have to execute every single idea I come up with – especially if it's to my own detriment. We have more time to pursue the things that are worth it than we think. Being overly proactive in all avenues of your life will not automatically make you successful, but it will make you regularly exhausted.

Stop wasting your focus

Don't worry, this isn't going to be a section on how to squeeze out every bit of concentration you have and put it in the right place. This is me reminding you that you are most likely giving too much attention to aspects of your career that don't deserve as much airtime. As a founder who spends a lot of time self-promoting online, I can honestly say that I spent far too much time worrying about my marketing and the engagement with my online content. Despite having grown a reputable career and position in the market, there's been many times where my energy and time have been stolen by focusing on the wrong metrics. You might not post social media content, but I'm sure you can think of a time where you've spent two weeks on something that could have been done in two days. You probably questioned yourself, delayed other things, or didn't rest properly because it was taking up too much of your thought process. It's this issue that we need to address. What things are you currently giving too much time to that could be compressed?

I interviewed Jennie Mc Ginn, an entrepreneur, who discovered just how much time she was wasting after she moved to a three-day working week. She told me: 'When we reduce our work weeks, there's always a pressure to compress it and fill it with as much work as possible, which is counterproductive. I don't want to work outside of those three days, so I have to figure out what I can handle, and I can't overcommit because I'll be burnt out.' Instead of pouring the same amount of hours into content creation for her business, Jennie now sets a time limit per week and vows to share whatever she creates in that window. If she wants to respect her own boundaries, she has to be less precious and more disciplined on tasks.

If you are responsible for managing your time, think about which things really require your extra attention and what can be streamlined to free up more time. In my own life, I realised that instead of posting five times a week on social media, I could pull back to two or three times and no one would notice. This will inevitably look different for everyone, but I have no doubt that there will be certain items on your to-do list that you can redirect time from in order to focus on the more important things in your life. A good question to reflect on, especially if you're a perfectionist, is: 'Will I care about this in a week, month or next year?' If not, do it quickly and move on.

In my conversation with the career coach Wendy O'Beirne, she shared the following questions that can really help us focus and centre on ourselves every day:

1. How am I feeling at the start of the day?
2. What do I need?
3. How do I want to feel at the end of the day?

I've found that by setting intentions for how I wanted to feel by the end of the day, I would base my decision-making on my answers. So, if I woke up feeling stressed about my workload, I knew I needed to move back deadlines, not take on any new requests and leave anything that could wait. Or if I woke up feeling tired, I knew I needed to be kinder to myself for not being able to work at the same pace and ask for someone else to support me.

Get out of the spotlight

If you're used to being very visible in your career and you're now feeling overstretched, this is your time to be asking yourself: 'How can I get out of the spotlight?' Again, this might feel counterproductive given that you have worked so hard to be recognised in your field, to be invited to things or to have a seat at the table, but the only way you can sustainably change without you feeling tempted to slip into your pre-existing work habits is to start phasing yourself out. This doesn't mean you need to reject every invite or opportunity, but it is about being extremely selective. I spoke to Sharmadean Reid, at the time the CEO of a tech start-up, who told me getting out of the spotlight has massively changed her relationship with work. After years of being visible and showing up to everything she possibly could, Sharmadean realised she'd got stuck in a world she didn't need to be in. She was so driven by what people or the press would say, that she was spending a lot of her time being visible and present in spaces that were draining her. She started pulling back, stopped attending everything she was invited to, and discovered very quickly that her reputation didn't dissipate overnight.

Doing this isn't always easy. As I've been writing this chapter, I have intentionally been trying to implement these insights, and getting out of the spotlight requires trusting that you have done a good enough job at cementing yourself already. You have to know your value in order to resist saying yes to things purely because you feel you may be missing out. I know some of you might be reading this thinking, 'I'm not well known enough to fade out, so doing this would hinder my career, not help it', but what I want you to be thinking more about is what you gain by stepping out of the spotlight – for me, that's time and emotional and physical energy.

Something I found to be useful when trialling this approach was writing a very clear list of rules that would help me to decide whether I should say yes or no to something. Below is the checklist for attending events that I would consult every time I was asked to be involved in something that required more energy than I had time to give:

Reasons to attend the event	Reasons not to attend
• Connect with people I don't have access to or couldn't meet 1:1 • It only happens annually • Genuinely interested in the topic and feel I would learn something new • I'm going through a quiet week or quiet period of work • It's not far to get to or the journey is fairly simple, inexpensive or enjoyable • I gain more from doing it than they do benefitting from me being there • There is a clear business opportunity that I would struggle to create	• My nervous system will be calmer as I'm not travelling • Better sleep as I'm not out of the house late, which means more rested • Rest my voice so I can protect it for my daily service (what I get paid for) • Eat healthier – no alcohol / proper meal at home so I feel better in my body • No fear of judgement – worrying about what other people are doing • Can focus on my priorities • I'm over-socialised – need time to myself

I often already knew the answer before going through these lists, but using them to confirm my final decision really put my mind at ease that I was doing the right thing for me at that point in time. Tapping out is like running. Most people don't love the activity itself, but they love the benefits that come from it: a clearer mind, higher energy, better sleeping and the ability to be more physically present. Taking yourself out of the spotlight works in exactly the same way. All that time you've been wasting in spaces you don't need to be in will become available for your use – however YOU want. Just because you get out of the spotlight doesn't mean your light will automatically dim – if anything it's likely to shine brighter because you'll finally be giving yourself the space you need.

Be a segmentor

Up until this point you might have spent your career merging both work and life. But a study from the American Psychological Association highlights that employees who disconnect from work during non-working hours actually experience better mental health and higher job performance.[14] Work-life expert Nancy Rothbard classifies people into two categories – integrators and segmentors. Integrators have a very strong desire to blur professional and personal life and have likely grown up in households where you've been surrounded by work-related conversations every night at the dinner table.[15] Segmentors, by contrast, keep their work and life mutually exclusive: when they are at work, they are 100 per cent at work and when they are at home, they are 100 per cent at home. Extreme examples of segmentors include people who intentionally have no photos of their family on their desks, insist on separating their work and home key chains, or won't bring spouses to work parties. In her research, Rothbard shares a story of a firefighter who would not wear his work clothes and boots to his house or hug his family until he had taken a bath. Not because of hygiene or cleanliness, but because he needed to separate himself from his working day in order to feel fully present at home. Rothbard argues there's a need for both integrators and segmentors in the workplace, but if you've found yourself compelled to action any of the points in this chapter, I'd be thinking about how segmenting might help with creating better boundaries – especially if you've become a remote worker and your living room has become your office, canteen and meeting room destination.

I spoke to a mum of three children who told me that in order to segment fully and be present with her kids, she proactively opted for a work phone that she could leave in the house when she's off the clock. She also stopped 'light working', as she realised sitting on her laptop with Netflix on did not count as switching off and, if anything, just extended how long a task was taking.

When we segment, we also create space for those around us to switch off from work, too. On a recent journey to see my family, I was reading a book all about personal branding. Every time I read something interesting, I would nudge my partner's arm, tell him to take out his headphones and read what I was pointing to. He did it the first time, but the second time he politely replied, 'I'm trying to switch off from work, it's a Sunday' and continued to listening to his podcast about an artist he admired. Normally I would have taken offence or felt like he wasn't showing enough of an interest, but I quickly recognised this was his version of segmenting and he was well within his right to remind me of his boundaries. As a self-confessed integrator, I can tell you it's not easy to change your habits, but instead of blurring the lines I want to focus on how you can create more separation. Here are a few examples that might inspire your own reflections:

- Can you have different work devices (separate laptop or phone for work vs leisure)?
- Can you create a start-of-day and end-of-day ritual (walks, scents, activities)?
- Can you have a no-devices rule in certain spaces or times of the day?
- Can you delete apps from your devices that you don't need?
- Can you change from work clothes to casual clothes?
- Can you opt for non-work-related content in your social and rest periods?
- Can you think of conversation points outside of the traditional work chat that might spark non-career-related conversations?

TOP TIP: *I spoke to Tamu Thomas, author of* Women Who Work Too Much, *and she recommended a three-step process that will help you segment your working day and attune to what you need:*

> **Morning:** First thing in the morning, we often get out of bed or wake up with our mind running. I want you to start taking charge of your day, before your day takes charge of you. When you first get out of bed, take a few breaths and ask yourself two questions: 'What do I need today?' and 'What do I want my day to feel like?' Allow yourself to sit with whatever comes up for you.
>
> **Lunch:** At least three times a week, I want you to have your lunch and just have lunch. No one hand on the keyboard, one ear listening to a podcast, no whatever – literally just have your

> lunch. It's called 'rest and digest' for a reason; when you're able to create space for restfulness, you start to feel safer in yourself. I say all the time, we live in the micro and these micro things we do throughout our day start to help us build trust.
>
> **End of day:** My final tip is, when you finish your workday, find a way to register with yourself that your day has ended. I've got an organic room spray that I spritz at the end of the day because the smell tells me I am finished. If you don't signal to your nervous system you have completed something, you'll just end up carrying it along through the rest of your day, giving it the power to disturb your sleep.

Find more time for solitude

Solitude is a word that rarely made it into my vocabulary, let alone my schedule, until recently, but this year I've been actively factoring it in. I, like many people, spend my life consuming external noise and content that is predominantly about bettering myself. Whether it's how to improve at work, how to improve my appearance, how to improve my relationships, or how to improve my sleep, almost all of the things I consume tell me I could be living my life better and more happily (though normally with the caveat that I need to purchase something). It's rare that we just spend time alone reflecting on what we actually need. As we've already covered in this chapter, part of that is because it can be uncomfortable to sit with our feelings. But I think another reason is because we see solitude as a lonely experience.

When I think of solitude I often think of solitary confinement: a form of imprisonment where an individual is kept in a prison cell alone with little or no contact with others. However, solitude in relation to rest is the opposite. As I've been processing a difficult year, having solitude has been a significant part of my healing process, and it's absolutely been the thing that has helped me to reframe my relationship with work. It's finding moments of stillness, low-stimulation and opportunities to drift off and daydream. It's going on walks, doing meditation, reading a book for fun – anything that allows you to find time to sit with yourself without distractions.

A couple of years ago I took a trip to Morocco, a five-day break staying at a remote wellness hotel with my partner surrounded by luscious gardens and beautiful weather. It was the perfect environment for practising solitude . . . except I made the classic mistake of not switching off my phone and regularly checking social media. On day two I found myself having an emotional meltdown as I saw that a peer in my industry had secured an impressive opportunity. Whilst I wanted to move on, it coincided with a time where I'd lost four opportunities in seven days, was feeling quite defeated and I spent the entire evening thinking about it. I was also annoyed that I was allowing it to affect me when I was meant to be on a break with my partner. Fortunately, I was able to talk it through with him, and by the end of the evening I felt lighter for voicing my emotions. Instead of switching off for the rest of the trip, however, I started thinking about how I could secure more business deals and more money when I returned – and not in an 'I'm-on-holiday-and-feel-so-inspired-way'. The truth was, I had gone into autopilot, obsessing over how I could get more even if I wasn't sure I really wanted it.

Since this trip and especially in the last few months, I've been intentionally thinking about how I can create more moments of solitude. Surprisingly, swimming has now become a weekly practice that I look forward to. At the start I used to think, 'God it would be great if you could get underwater headphones so you can listen to music or podcasts whilst you swim' (I later found out these were available online), but as I continued to go, I realised that I didn't want or need noise. Whether it's ten minutes with your morning coffee or on your walk home from the bus stop, make sure you give yourself enough time and space, away from any external noise, to sit with your thoughts. Ask yourself:

- When can I have a moment of uninterrupted stillness?
- How can I make this a habit?
- What activities can I do that create a barrier between me and the external world?

Tapping Out: Changing Directions

Now we've explored tapping out in your full-time role, let's dive into how you can adopt the same mindset when you're considering switching careers or starting something new. Whether you're looking to move jobs, launch a new business, or even shake up your client or customer base to better align with your refreshed outlook on life, the next few tips will help guide you towards making choices that feel more in tune with *you* and what you really want.

View your career as a body of work

I attend a monthly event series that celebrates talent in the creative industry. Each time they select speakers from different fields (photography, art, film, illustration, etc.) to present their work to the audience. Although their craft is completely unique and different, the one thing they have in common is that they describe their output as 'a body of work' and it's something I want you to consider adopting, too. A body of work is defined as the entirety of the creative or academic output produced by a particular unit or individual. The phrase is commonly used by artists to describe a long project or your practice in total, and generally conveys a message central to your identity as an artist. Poonam Dhuffer, an artist, somatic coach and visionary, told me that she believes a body of work is an evolutionary process that grows in relation to your inner and outer worlds and grows with you as an individual, with each thing you create representing a different patchwork in the tapestry of the whole. Each piece represents all the facets of life weaving in and out. I remember hearing these words and thinking how calming it would be to consider your career trajectory as a body of work, or as a summary of everything you do in your life, rather than as something linear. A body of work is something that grows with you as an individual, with each thing that you create representing a different branch or moment in your life.

In this light, it's much easier to give yourself the grace and permission to follow your genuine interests in your working life, rather than feeling chained to the rat race. There shouldn't be any shame in not sticking to one thing, as you're not falling behind if you choose to change paths; you're just adding to your portfolio of experiences. Musicians and actors make genre shifts all the time without a second thought. Beyoncé's last few albums have seamlessly covered everything from R&B to house and even country, whilst Tom Hanks went from playing Forrest Gump to voicing Woody in *Toy Story* to starring in *Captain Phillips*. And when they switch it up, no one bats an eye or calls them indecisive. In fact, we celebrate their versatility and ability to show up in so many different ways. The beauty of their careers isn't measured by what they do week to week or year to year; it's about the big picture, their body of work as a whole. It's about growth and reinvention, and we applaud them for it. Just like you should applause yourself for it, too.

So what if the next few years of your career aren't life-changingly great or noteworthy. It doesn't mean that will come to define your entire body of work. If you need to take a job to help secure a mortgage because having a house is what you really want right now, do it. If you get a chance to do something once in your lifetime but it stops your upwards career trajectory, do it. Or if, like me, you have a year where the best thing you feel you did was survive something really difficult, be proud that you made it through, and trust that your body of work will be stronger when you feel it too.

Analyse your location

Before committing to a new opportunity or tying yourself down to certain time zone, I want you to reflect on whether you need to change your environment if you want to stick to tapping out. I've always been a city person but, as someone who currently lives in London, there's no denying that it can be all-consuming, hyper-stimulating and financially difficult. I often joke that I can't step out of my apartment in London without spending a minimum of £20, even on a walk around the park. It only takes me being on a train for thirty minutes in the opposite direction, surrounded by green fields, for me to quickly realise just how much energy living in a major city consumes and to question if that's really what I want.

I spoke to Sharmadean Reid, who relocated from London to a city in the midlands, who told me that her decision was prompted by her need for both literal and financial breathing space. She said everyone she knew would always be escaping London with weekends away booked or spending so much money on wellness just to cope with living in the city. Changing locations allowed Sharmadean to tap out of a formal structure she'd been working in. She has more capacity to create in her career because she isn't as distracted or consumed by the daily city life, whilst also being able to do the school run and spend more time with family who live nearby.

Journalist Helen Russell similarly describes leaving London in an article for *Stylist* magazine.[16] After her partner secured a job in rural Denmark, Helen and her husband visited the country to get a flavour of what she'd be swapping her life for: 'We caught a glimpse of a different way of life. People walked more slowly. They took their time, stopping, sometimes, to take in their surroundings. Or just . . . breathe. They looked relaxed.' When they eventually made the move, she admitted she still felt pangs of jealousy seeing colleagues being promoted, but ultimately realised she could sleep well now and that she no longer had a stress knot in her stomach. Now, I'm not expecting you to read this and swap your busy life for a hygge-life tomorrow, but what I am encouraging you to think about is which location will allow you to thrive the most. And when I say thrive, I don't mean climbing the career ladder. I mean, where will *you* flourish?

Exploring new places and getting out of your routine also allows you to meet new people and find communities that you really connect with. Over the last year, I've been travelling to New York to spread the F*ck Being Humble movement Stateside, and every time I've visited, I've felt an energy shift of optimism, excitement and openness. Of course it was hectic, it's the city that never sleeps, but I felt welcomed with open arms by everyone I met. I also got to experience awe daily, an emotion that rarely pops up in my routine when I'm home. Every time I returned to the UK I was reminded of our cynical, reserved and pessimistic qualities, and just how much it drains you, especially when you're trying to grow a business.

Additionally, working in a new country or location outside of what you already know might encourage you to get out and step away from your work more. When I moved to Paris for six months with my partner, I found that our excitement to explore the city everyday meant that I naturally was better at maintaining healthier work boundaries. It was one of the best periods of my life, despite being the year my company earned the least. So, if you're taking this time to think about what you want next, I urge you to think about how your surroundings could possibly play a part.

- What currently drains you about your environment?
- What would you like more of?
- What is missing?
- Where have you felt a connection to a place?
- What would you gain if you changed your location?

You don't have to chase love

I'm sure the career gurus reading this book will hate me for saying this, but you don't need to love the job you choose, you just need to love the life the job pays for. In the Stick and Twist chapters, we explored how to reconnect with work and do more of what you want, but now I think it's time for me to remind you that you don't have to be OBSESSED with your career to hold down a happy life. In fact, if you want to be more of a segmentor than integrator, doing something that you're not completely infatuated with might help you to keep a healthy distance from it.

In an article for the *Guardian*, psychologist Tessa West wrote about 'Why it's OK not to love your job'; she argued that many of us never actually find love with our career, though we are thoroughly convinced everyone else has.[17] She goes on to explain that those of us who do manage to find it are not necessarily immune from negative outcomes such as chronic stress and burnout. Love means dedicating your whole self to the job and, in turn, feeling every failure and setback like a punch to the gut. She recommends that we should kiss the 'love' trope goodbye and instead try to have a healthy amount of psychological distance from work.

When you love your job, it can be easy to find yourself working extra hours without being paid, overcommitting and feeling the need to be best in the game. Just being content with your career, however, creates a different dynamic. If you compare it to dating, you can see how the time and energy you dedicate to someone might change if you're completely and utterly in love with them vs having a more casual relationship. Instead of exhausting yourself searching for the one, it could be healthier to accept that your job can't love you back. This is not to say that if you've found the thing you adore you should give it up, but more a note to remember that our job doesn't have to fulfil our human need of desire. I know a lot of people who are content with their work and don't spend hours offloading about it to me every time I see them, and, truthfully, I don't think it's a bad relationship to have.

- What job would you do if you weren't focused on loving it?
- What can you tolerate?
- What have been the downfalls of loving your job?

Choose a less demanding job

This might be hard for the overachievers to read, but after years of always looking for 'more of a challenge' at work, it might now be

CAREER COMEDOWN

time to change your working conditions. It might feel scary changing roles, industries, or even feel like you're taking a step down, but if your work conditions are not conducive to how you want to live your life and there isn't much flexibility in the system you're working in, a change in environment might be exactly what you need. If you've ever used the excuses: 'That's just what it's like in the industry I work in' or 'Everyone's expected to work like that' then you know sticking to your current place of work isn't going to help you to tap out.

During my interviews with successful tap-outers, one of the common changes people made was taking on roles that didn't require too much from them or that were less overwhelming than what they were doing before. Sophie Rogozinska, for example, wanted to move from working in production into becoming a website designer, and needed a job that didn't leave her feeling exhausted or distracted during the transition. She figured out how much she needed to earn to cover her essentials and took on a part-time job in a coffee shop to pay for her living costs. From a financial perspective it gave her the security to pursue her new direction, but more importantly she loved having absolutely no responsibilities or stress that she'd carry home with her. She found she could do her job well and still have energy at the end of the day to focus on what she actually cared about in her future.

Another person I spoke to was feeling extremely burnt out after struggling to sustain their freelance design career, so she decided to take on a part-time job in a supermarket. Choosing a shift-based role was better than working in an environment that insisted she jumped through every hoop to prove her worth, when she really needed time to recuperate and feel more like herself again. For clarity, I'm not saying that either of these roles don't have demanding elements to them, but in both situations they offered a change in pace of working and each person felt they had more capacity as a result.

Another way to reframe a less demanding job is to ask: 'What comes easy to me?' It sounds simple, but many of us still believe work has to be gruelling to be valid. I've heard older generations mock content creators calling it 'not a real job', often out of resentment from having done work that felt more time-consuming or less glamorous. But just because something is hard doesn't mean it's more worthy. I recently helped a new mum plan her freelance comeback. When I suggested a higher rate for a service she's great at, she said, 'I can't charge that, it's too easy.' I stopped her right there: 'That's exactly why you should charge more.' This conversation feeds into the mindset that if it's not extremely demanding or difficult, we don't see it as proper work. We need to shake the mindset that ease equals low value. Instead, ask: 'What's the value of my skill? Who needs it most? How can I charge more for what I do best?'

I also spoke to Lisa O'Hare, a tax specialist who had gone from working at a massive corporate business to part time at a smaller business. Due to her schedule being less crammed, she found she had time to reconnect with her creative side and started doing art classes at her local community centre every Monday, before deciding to put on a show at the Greater Manchester Fringe Festival. 'I had always been to comedy and theatre shows all my life, so I thought, that's my marathon,' she said. It was so successful she went on to host a show at the iconic Edinburgh Fringe Festival aged forty-seven. Lisa felt like she was having a second life as a poet which has led her to all sorts of amazing opportunities.

If you don't want to play the game of working overtime without compensation, or feel guilt-tripped to go above and beyond every minute of the day, could you instead choose a career or profession that makes it harder for you to continue those unhealthy habits?

What jobs have specific set working hours? What jobs can you only do in your place of work (and not at home at 9 p.m.)? What jobs don't expect you to be available 24/7? What jobs only expect you to do one thing instead of juggling a hundred things all at once? Remember, as we've already discussed, everything is a trade-off, so making this switch might not give you that jump-out-of-bed work purpose feeling, but maybe it will enable you to jump out of bed and enjoy life beyond work. So now I want you to reflect on:

- If you were to take on a less demanding job, what could it be?
- What working conditions do you need or want?
- What will this give you more time for?

Sell your expertise, not your time

As mentioned earlier in this chapter, more people are seeking ways to 'work smarter, not harder'. The concept is based on the premise that you don't have to work longer hours to get the results or money you want – instead you should prioritise becoming as efficient as possible. This might mean moving from charging your time at hourly rates to an output-based fee or finding ways to package your expertise into a sellable product that can create a passive income stream. This option is for people who are done working for other people (clients or companies) and want to sell their knowledge instead. Rather than being a designer that works forty hours a week for a company, a design consultant would create a much shorter offer: perhaps a one-hour talk, a one-day workshop, or possibly offer three hours a month on a retainer. The key thing is that the client is no longer paying for output – they are paying for knowledge instead.

I spoke to Jennie, a brand and marketing specialist who has been transitioning into a working-less-but-charging-more model. She said: 'I no longer want to be on the executional side of things, I want to be in a strategic role where you don't need me every day. I'm not freelancing, slotting into everyone else's needs anymore or involving myself in other companies. I just want a lifestyle business. I don't want to scale it up, I want to scale it right back.' To do this, she has moved from a 1:1 service of freelancing to a 1:many model, where she sells a singular product on personal branding promoted on her website. She's also decided she's only working Monday to Wednesday and has a take it or leave it attitude when it comes to new work – if it doesn't fit her terms, she's not doing it anymore. Whilst living this way isn't an option for everyone, Jennie has found that it works to give her what she truly wants, which is more time with her children.

For the people who already sell their expertise, it might be worth reflecting on your prices. When I spoke to a founder who runs a membership platform that aims to advance women in the workplace, she realised that what she was offering was extremely high value for the price per person. Her commitment to the cause of accelerating women and her desire to create something commercially appealing meant she was over-giving. Great for her community members, but not great for her as she was overstretched and burning out from delivering it. She decided to pull back on what was included as she realised there was still a significant amount of value if she cut the membership offering by 50 per cent. Now she has done this, she's freed up more time to explore her life outside of work and still retained a healthy amount of community members.

So how can you implement this in your own career? Let's run

through a few different job types and how they could swap working a traditional eight-hour working day for shorter bursts of work:

- Book Editor > Could offer to review manuscripts, book proposals or do weekly check-ins with authors
- Teacher > Could offer tutoring, online digital courses, downloadable guides
- Sales Assistant > Could create sales training videos, speak at events, deliver training to local stores
- Designer / Writer / Creator > Offer package deals, where it's not based on the hours in but based on output

And if you're not sure there is an appetite for your particular expertise, I'd encourage you to think about which other areas you could train up in. As I said earlier, the common misconception is that you have to be doing something for ten-plus years before you can confidently start charging for your expertise on it, but actually sometimes all it takes is a different angle, USP or niching down on a topic.

For example, if you spent every day for the next six months studying every video format on social media that could help drive sales, there is no reason why you couldn't package up the insights studied into some form of digital product and sell it. Yes, you might need to work on your marketing and show the behind-the-scenes of you doing this, but people don't just buy your expertise because of mastery, they also buy it for convenience. Most business owners don't have time to spend on researching how social media could improve their businesses themselves, but would, if marketed well enough, spend £1000 on attending a one-day training course on it. A big part of selling your expertise is simply knowing where the demand lies, picking a price point that is healthy enough to attract customers and sustain you, and having the willingness to promote yourself. I don't want anyone to be disillusioned and think that if you do this, you'll be sitting on a yacht sipping cocktails every month but, if you want to break away from the traditional nine-to-five working world, selling your expertise could be a viable option. Think about:

- How could you teach your skillset to others?
- If you were going to make an online product using your skills, what could it be?

Living your best (*ordinary*) life

Before we end this chapter, I wanted to share one final thought that might help change your relationship with work – and that is, that it's okay to live an ordinary life. I know that's not how social media makes you feel, what life coaches will tell you or what brands want you to believe, but for anyone who needs to hear this: your life doesn't need to feel or look like a movie. I'm all for chasing dreams and living your life fully, but maybe a full life doesn't have to come from having a glossy career. Maybe all we actually need is to chase contentment.

I felt so comforted when I saw a TikTok video that said: 'I'm sat in the car eating a Subway at a service station and this is the most exciting thing that's going to happen to me all week, and I'm okay with that.' I'm not sure if my phone was listening in on my conversations or could sense my personal life was unravelling, but that video found me at a time when I needed to hear those words. This last year has been the hardest of my entire existence on Earth, and the things that have meant the most to me have been the ordinary moments. Sitting on my sofa snuggled up in duvet, watching my favourite Netflix shows or laughing so much with my friends it begins to hurt. It's been walking to the local coffee shop without feeling overwhelmed or overstimulated. And it's been feeling safe in my mind and my body. I finally get the thing parents have been saying for years: that it's not about the things you buy or what you consume, it's all the moments in between. It's about finding small pockets of calm in a world full of chaos.

In the final episode of Dolly Alderton's TV adaptation of *Everything I Know About Love*, the mother of the teenage daughter tries to reassure her about dating, saying, 'I think that you are looking for an extraordinary kind of love, but I don't think, for what it's worth, that you want to be loved in an extraordinary way. I think what you want, is to be loved plainly and quietly, without spectacle or anxiety.[18] Those words resonated with me deeply. We can all think of a time where our obsession with chasing a plot twist or being the main character of the story didn't always result in feeling our best selves. If you've got to this point in the book, it could in fact be because what you're chasing isn't actually fireworks or drama, but the validation that living an ordinary life is acceptable. I know it might not always feel like it, but more people are living ordinary lives than you think; it's important that you recognise that it's not only an option for you, it might be the thing you actually need.

Interview Spotlight

Meena Alexander spent ten years as a journalist and, at the time of this interview, had just resigned from her position of associate editor at Stylist *magazine to go travelling for nine months.*

Was there a specific moment you realised something needed to change?

I've probably been going too hard in my career for quite a few years, and I've only ever been praised for that. I've got lots out of overworking, so I thought it was all worth it. But towards the end of 2023, there was a moment where I had to call my boss and tell them I was struggling and needed to slow down a little bit. She was really shocked and couldn't believe I'd got to such an extreme point of stress and had been hiding it. I was instantly told to take time off and do what I needed. It was then that I realised I was the one putting this on myself, no one else. I couldn't even make out that it's because I've got the most stressful job ever and have all these demands, actually most of this pressure is coming from me. I needed to work out why that is and how to take my foot off the gas a little bit. I'm not a heart surgeon, I'm a journalist for a magazine, and so you almost feel like you're not allowed to take those breaks or have those boundaries around something that's supposed to be fun.

What has helped with your own mindset to allow you switch things up?

If I'm being honest, I've always wanted to experience a different culture. I knew it would be temporary as I'd planned to build my life in London, but having time to experience something new was important to me. I am really ambitious and being able to say I am an editor felt quite important to me, but now I'm in a high position in my career, I feel like I've earned permission to follow my other dreams.

The other factor was burnout and being able to see exactly what would happen if I kept going at the same pace. When I asked myself, 'What am I getting out of this?' my answer was nothing, apart from feeling bad about myself and having nothing to give to the other areas of my life. Once you've seriously planted that seed in your mind, things start unfolding quite quickly. You start to think about everything differently. At work, I started having all sorts of questions in my head: Do I want to take on this big project or should I start delegating and sharing it with my colleagues if I might not be here to finish it? Am I going to start saving? Do I need to start living slightly differently? I found that when I made that decision, everything in my life got easier very quickly, in that I had a goal and something to save towards. I also wanted to spend real quality time with my friends and family because I was going to be away for a few months.

I had given myself permission to take my foot off the gas and in doing that, I realised I'm still doing my job well. No one's turning around and thinking she's got lazy or she's doing terrible work all of a sudden. It's frustrating to learn that so late in the day, but it is a good lesson to learn that you don't have to give 100 per cent to be good at your job.

What trends do you see happening in relation to our relationships with work?

I'm part of this massive group of people that know the way we're working isn't sustainable, but we don't actually know what the solution is. So we're going to step out of the stream for a little while and figure it out. In the next few years, I think people will be a lot more focused on purpose and how a job makes us feel rather than how it looks and our external status. I also think community is a huge thing that we're missing in our lives in so many ways. We've been forced to think about our careers as this individualistic-climb-the-ladder approach rather than reflecting on whether we're working with the kind of people that inspire us. The same goes for outside of our work: Do you feel like you've got an important role in your community, your family or your network?

What are some of the things that have helped you separate your identity from work?

I have gone from reading newspapers and magazines practically every day to only reading novels. Originally, I said it was just temporary because I love journalism, but it has massively helped in that I'm not constantly thinking, 'How would I have written about that?' Or 'Should I be covering that?' You just get to enjoy something creatively, it's having some impact on you, but you're just taking it in and your brain's not worrying.

I also journal and I find it really useful for reflecting on how I'm thinking differently about things that I'm worried about. When I started writing in my journal after I'd quit my job, I expected to be apprehensive, but I felt like a different person whilst writing straightaway. I can see that I've got a lot more headspace and I'm excited about the future;

I thought I'd be nervous about the unknown, but it feels really nice not to know what's coming up because that means there's no checkpoints or goals that I can or can't achieve this year. There's no way of failing or not succeeding, the point is just to exist.

What's one thing you wish people remembered on their journey to tapping out?

I would just zoom out and reflect on how long your working life is going to be. Do you really want to work constantly to the point where you don't have anything but crumbs to give to your other areas of life until your retirement age? Or isn't it much more valuable to learn about yourself now, and savour all the joy, and as early as you can?

You've got more time than you think. Attitudes are changing – people aren't going to penalise you for having a less than traditional sort of career trajectory or life trajectory. There are so many decisions you can make that you could regret, but I have literally never heard a woman in her eighties go, 'I wish I hadn't spent those three months travelling around the world.'

Tap Out - Final Thoughts

As I wrap up this section of the book, I really want you to think about how much of your identity is tied to your career and whether that's truly serving you. Many of us get caught up in the idea that our job defines us, but what happens if we step back and reflect on where that belief might be causing harm? Are you caught in a cycle of being hyper-productive, hyper-independent or constantly overachieving? It's time to take a look at these patterns and ask yourself whether work has become an unhealthy source of validation, pushing you to overdo it at the expense of your well-being. I am saying all of this with genuine compassion and care and, although it might make you feel a little vulnerable acknowledging your journey to this point, I promise you it's worth it in the end.

My main hope for writing this chapter is to emphasise to you that your worth isn't defined by your job or career achievements. You are valuable simply because you exist, not because of your title or accomplishments. It's something I wish we heard more of in society, and I'll keep shouting it from the rooftops until I'm blue in the face. I keep coming back to these words from Wayne Dyer: 'Peace is the result of retraining your mind to process life as it is, rather than how you think it should be.' When we begin to accept this, we free ourselves from the need to constantly prove ourselves in our career. We can stop playing the 'hero' at the office, break free from toxic cycles, and start living in a way that doesn't require giving 110 per cent all the time. Honestly, doesn't that sound like a breath of fresh air?

Whether or not you choose to tap out, I truly believe it's incredibly valuable to take a moment and imagine a life where work doesn't dominate every decision. As someone who's been actively practising this whilst writing this chapter, I can tell you firsthand that I've seen some amazing benefits already:

- I get to the end of each month with joyful memories.
- I'm not feeling burnt out, exhausted or regretful.
- I'm not resenting commitments I've made, because I'm filling my cup elsewhere.

- I'm trying things I haven't done before (even doing it alone) and being okay with being a TERRIBLE beginner again!
- I'm moving away from my negative habits, and I'm feeling more connected to my body and better rested.
- I'm fitting work around my life vs my life around my work.

Not every year of our lives needs to be packed with major achievements to be meaningful. I wish more people realised that, in certain seasons of life, stepping back from work isn't just a smart move, it's one you'll look back on and thank yourself for. Sometimes, the most fulfilling path is the one where you choose simplicity, peace and balance, focusing on what genuinely makes you happy rather than chasing the flawless, curated life you see online.

CHAPTER 6
POST-AUDIT

So now we've been through all your options, I think it's important that you give yourself a more thorough career audit. At the start of reading this book you might have been feeling frazzled, hopeless, or been suffering with a lack of clarity about what you want to come next. Now, I hope you have a better understanding of what has led you to the point of career comedown and how you need to combat it. You have stories to learn from and options to choose from. This is your time to really process everything you've read.

The following audit is a collection of questions that will help you reflect on the career and kind of life you want to work towards:

Mindset

- What things do you need to unlearn to move forward?
- What beliefs about your current situation are holding you back?
- What beliefs about other people are you letting influence your decisions?
- Where do you feel you are currently settling?
- What stories are you telling yourself that might be stopping you from moving forward?

- What is your past self telling your future self?
- What mistakes do you not want to make again?
- What situations can't you change, but you could change your beliefs around?

Confidence

- What value do you bring to the table?
- How can you measure success without external input?
- Where are you currently hiding or dimming yourself?
- How are your work surroundings affecting your confidence?
- What gives you a full-body yes feeling?
- When are you at your most resourceful?
- What are some of the moments you've felt most confident?
- What was a decision you made that you didn't regret? What does this tell you about what you need?

Communication

- What is your career love language?
- What do you need to ask for more of?
- What boundaries do you need to set in place?
- What boundaries could you have flexibility with?
- What do you need to change about the way you speak about work to yourself and others?
- What do you need to say no to?
- What conversations do you need to have that you are avoiding?

POST-AUDIT

Identity

- What are your top five values?
- How much of your identity is linked to your career?
- How would you define and measure wealth in your world?
- If you didn't centre your life around work, what would it look like?
- What type of role model do you want to be? And who to?
- What external values do you need to let go of?
- Who is living the life you admire? Can you describe what you think it is to live that life?

Letting Go

- What dreams do you need to let go of?
- What is the cost of you playing it safe?
- In five years' time, what decision would you be happy you made?
- What have you learned about yourself through this experience, even if it didn't go as planned?

Pride

- If someone asked you to describe your career, what would you feel proud of right now?
- If you were to start from scratch or pivot in your career, what's a new story you'd feel proud to tell?
- Outside of work, what would you feel proud of doing, maintaining or achieving?

- What would a younger version of you be proud of pursuing?
- What things have you been conditioned to take pride in, that you might no longer resonate with?

Time

- What changes do you need to make to protect your time?
- What are you currently missing out on?
- Where are you giving too much effort professionally?
- How can you segment your working day from your personal life?
- Where can you create more time for solitude?
- What is taking too much of your focus?
- What is urgent and what can wait?
- If you knew you had limited time left, what would you change?
- What happens if you do nothing?

Ambitions

- What are you willing to trade off or deprioritise?
- What is on your career bucket list?
- What is on your personal bucket list?
- What limitations do you need to be more accepting of?
- What do you not want to regret in the future?
- What ambitions can wait in this season of your life?
- When is enough, enough?
- When you think about your ideal position, how does that differ from now?

Connection

- What support is missing that you need?
- Who is draining you?
- Where do you feel respected?
- What do you need to ask for help with?
- Whose opinion do you value?
- Who is affected if you don't make changes?

Joy

- Where is the enjoyment in what you do?
- If you had to do something unpaid for the rest of your life, what would it be?
- How can you increase the play in your life?
- Where and who do you go to for inspiration?
- Where do you find calm and safety?
- What are you craving?
- What would it take to have your ideal day?
- What are the small moments of joy you can find in each day?

CHAPTER 7
WHAT'S NEXT?

I appreciate that we've delved into a lot in this book, and I also know from experience that it can feel overwhelming to know where to start making changes. To help with this, I thought I'd recap what you can do over the next month, six months and year for all three options.

First 30 Days

Stick: If you're choosing to stick, it's time to get a work diary or planner so you can document what is and isn't working for you. Start with these questions: Why did you first get into this industry? What excited you about it? What was the vision you had when you started? Now, think about where things may have gone off-track. How has your direction shifted along the way? Is it the pace of meetings, workload, people, your space or the quality of what you're working on? What you wanted back when you first started might look different to what you want now – what has changed about your goals and expectations, and what, if anything, has stayed the same? By asking these questions, you can start to untangle your journey to this point. Then,

I want you to write a summary of each day at work and start to spot patterns in what's lighting you up and what's draining you.

Twist: You can't twist if you don't know where you are going, so for the next thirty days I want you to tune in to the things you're feeling drawn to for your new adventure. Narrow it down to a couple of routes and start looking into the process of starting that new beginning. It's useful to look into job roles, industry needs and market opportunities; really do your research on how and where you might be able to move to next. Doing this will help you to understand what your exit strategy timeline is. For some of you, you might need to stick out your current situation until you build up some funds in the bank, or you might need to spend some time speaking to people who have made similar moves. The point is we want to avoid a rushed decision and give you enough time to find some clarity before committing to something permanent.

Tap Out: For the next thirty days, I want you to intentionally reflect on what it is you are tapping out of. What habits, patterns or behaviours might you need to address if you want to commit to tapping out? Don't worry, you don't need to have all the answers just yet – this is more of an observation stage. Think about things that you might be distracted from. When would you like to be more present (but you're currently not)? Or reflect on the cost of staying in your current situation – what cost does that have on other aspects of your life? This period is for you to assess where you might be stretching yourself too thin and what you could gain if you weren't giving your all to work. I also want you to be more inquisitive with others on how they manage their work-life balance: speak to people about what they are prioritising and how they're juggling it all (or aren't) and be open to seeing other people's perspectives that don't mirror your own.

2–6 Months

Stick: After you've identified the areas that have dipped and, more importantly, why they have, we need to start exploring the changes you can make to align your career more closely to your preferences. This is your research period: the time where you look into how people have done what you're hoping to do. I want you to study their strategies, ask for their guidance, or read up on techniques that can help prepare you to make those changes. It's not that difficult to pinpoint the problem areas, but I want you to think about solutions. Get more intel on the company you work for or the clients you work with and learn more about the direction they're going in, their needs and their requirements. Can you align your preferences with what they're looking for or might you need to look at a different approach?

Twist: Now you've got a more considered direction that you want to work towards, it's time to start working on the reinvention strategy. During this period, you should be pulling together everything you need to feel confident and comfortable with making the transition. This might be a mixture of upskilling, reframing your marketing materials, updating or creating new online channels and building out the funds you need to keep going. These are your test-drive months and might look like doing pro-bono work in the field, volunteering, joining community groups, networking, reading up on the industry or self-initiating activities that will help to reposition you in the best way. The goal is to sample what you'll be doing and to prepare everything you need so that you can fully embody this new version of you before taking the leap.

Tap Out: Given the categories we discussed of being high achieving, hyper-productive and fiercely independent, there's a strong chance that when you've observed your own bad habits you'll want to implement drastic changes straight away. But I'd encourage you to start looking at small ways you can start exploring your identity outside of work, before you commit to a complete overhaul of your career. It might be doing classes on a weekend that you've always wanted to do or doing the school run to help you feel more connected to parenthood. Whatever it is, let's start introducing some of the things you wish you were doing more of. The reason it's important to ease yourself into this process is because sometimes we fantasise about other ways of living only to discover that's not what we were missing. So, before you begin the process of elimination, focus on identifying and exploring some of the things you think will bring you more joy.

WHAT'S NEXT?

6–12 Months

Stick: By this point you will have spent a good amount of time reflecting on what you feel is missing and doing research on ways to change it. Now it's about implementing your learnings and making them stick. This is where setting your boundaries, preparing clear responses and intentionally speaking up for what you do and don't want to be doing will come in. Have your ways of working document and your list of questions to help you measure your own happiness ready. Remember things can take a while to change and shift so if you don't feel like you've reached your end goal yet, be patient and document the small steps you are taking to reclaim your career.

Twist: Once you've got your funds and you've come to the end of your exit strategy process, this is your moment to step forward and own your new direction. As discussed in the Twist chapter, regular self-promotion and storytelling will be needed as you move through your next chapter, as you'll still be in the process of building trust with others. You will have your taxi pitch ready, and you'll be nicely integrating yourself into the space you'll be working in. Networking during this time will continue to be important and having an openness to saying yes to things that feel scary or unknown is essential. Remember: we don't want to be carrying any old and unhelpful habits into this new period, so keep your options open and don't have your heart set on one outcome just yet. You might need to do some career zig-zagging and jump feet first into opportunities that come your way.

Tap Out: Hopefully through adding more of what you need into your situation, you'll start to see what you now need to subtract to sustain a more enjoyable life. Your decisions will not be made with a career first mindset, instead you will be implementing a life-centred approach. At this stage, you will become more selective with who and what you let in, and your moments of solitude will be protected at all costs. You might still feel pangs of fear or worry that you're being left behind, but you fill in those gaps with more nourishing things. You will start to explore which parts of your working life can survive with less of your energy and accept that you don't always need to save the day. And you will need to keep adding people into your network who are moving through life in similar ways, so you feel the emotional support from others to keep persevering. Regular check-ins with yourself will be important to ensure all of your efforts are contributing to the exact kind of life you want.

CONCLUSION

As I reflect on my journey of writing this book, I can honestly say it has been *life changing*. I always knew I'd find analysing my own relationship with work confronting because instead of chasing the next shiny thing, it meant I would have to hit pause and do some deep introspection. At points, I've felt exposed, frustrated and surprised at my own revelations. There was one specific writing day from this process where I was having total creative block, and I panicked, telling my friend that I couldn't do it.

She replied:

'Stef, there's a reason you are working on this project right now. It has come to you at this chapter in your life for a purpose. Even if the unknown feels scary, you'll get there.'

I smiled, nodded, and knew that she was right.

Like many of you reading this book, I have been on autopilot, chasing, climbing, hustling and moving towards things that didn't always align with me in my career. I have said yes to FAR too many things I knew in my gut weren't right; I've not vocalised my preferences, got hung up on measuring all the wrong things, and not always been honest with myself on what I really wanted, or needed. I've been scared to step forward, to be seen as a beginner, and have been pretty tunnel vision for the last ten years. I've been surrounding myself with people who think and work similarly to me, so I haven't been pushed to question my approach – if anything I've just been celebrated for overworking. And that's why writing this book hasn't just been a project to help others, it's the book I've needed without knowing it.

When I wrote my first book, *F*ck Being Humble*, I was so eager to help people kick down doors and get what they deserved, I didn't realise that my own 'Career Comedown' was in motion. I didn't envisage needing to write this book because like the rest of you, I assumed that if you follow the career track and do everything right, you'll feel complete. I guess at that point I didn't realise just how much our lives and our preferences can (and will) change. If anyone knows how it feels to be disconnected from your career, it's me. It can be all consuming, draining and leave you feeling hopeless. Which is why I set out to write a book that would not just simplify the process, it would help you implement it, too. I wanted to provide you with a singular space where you could see all your options in one place, have a chance to weigh them up and uncover what it takes to make them a reality.

Additionally, I wanted to show you that you *do* have options. Your story doesn't have to stand still where it is right now. You can:

1. **Stick**
2. **Twist**
3. **Tap Out**

I think it's important for me to say that you can do all three steps, and in any order you want. Just because you decide to *Stick* for the next three years doesn't mean you can't be exploring ways to *Tap Out* at the same time. And even if you decided to *Twist* and then realise you made the wrong call, you can always go back to your old career and follow the steps to sticking. If there's one

CONCLUSION

thing I've always said, it's that there is no one-size-fits-all approach to this process. And there shouldn't be. How boring would it be if all our lives were books with the exact same start, middle and end? What I really want you to remember is that you have the freedom to choose. Yes, some options might need more time and planning, but the despair you might have been feeling before you picked up this book shouldn't be a permanent state of mind. Just as my friend said to me, there's a reason you were attracted to this book and it's because you want to see changes in your story.

I don't want you to lose yourself in your career and become unrecognisable. I don't want you to question your worth and keep pondering, 'Is this it?' I want you to find something that lights you up and allows you to live the life you want to live. For some of you that might mean tackling those difficult conversations head on, saying no to people and being more intentional. Others of you might be redefining work for yourselves altogether. Whatever you do, I just want you to find a solution that gets YOU closer to what you really want.

If writing this book has taught me anything it's that when we are at full capacity, overspilling or overwhelmed by external noise, we don't make decisions that make sense for us. We avoid things, we take short cuts and disassociate from ourselves. I don't want this for you. I want you to know there is a version of work that can work for you, but only if you have the courage to find it.

ENDNOTES

Introduction

1. 'Precarious pay and uncertain hours'. The Living Wage. 2023. Available at: https://www.livingwage.org.uk/sites/default/files/2023-08/Precarious%20pay%20and%20uncertain%20hours%20-%202023%20%281%29.pdf.
2. 'How the US job landscape is changing – and how to adapt'. McKinsey Global Institute. 2024. Available at: https://www.mckinsey.com/mgi/overview/in-the-news/how-the-us-job-landscape-is-changing-and-how-to-adapt.
3. Eleanor Kaye, 'Why you should make a career lattice rather than climbing the ladder'. *Stylist* magazine. 2023. Available at: https://www.stylist.co.uk/life/careers/why-you-need-career-champion-work-mentor/818565.

Chapter 1: What is Career Comedown?

1. 'Gen Z Is Toxic for Companies, Employers Believe'. *Newsweek*. 2024. Available at: https://www.newsweek.com/employers-say-gen-z-toxic-workplace-1882557#:~:text=The%20criticism%20for%20Gen%20Z,and%20toxicity%20in%20the%20workplace.
2. 'Why Gen Z Workers Want It All'. *BBC News*. 2022. Available at: https://www.linkedin.com/pulse/why-gen-z-workers-want-all-bbc-news/.
3. 'Young adults have lowest life satisfaction, says Harvard study. Happiness at work can fix it'. *ThePrint*. 2023. Available at: https://theprint.in/feature/young-adults-have-lowest-life-satisfaction-says-harvard-study-happiness-at-work-can-fix-it/1763323/.
4. 'Workplace burnout is on the rise – here's why'. *Business Post*. Available at: https://www.businesspost.ie/irish-tatler/workplace-burnout-is-on-the-rise-heres-why/.

ENDNOTES

5. 'What actions are people taking because of the rising cost of living?' *Office for National Statistics*. 2022. Available at: https://www.ons.gov.uk/peoplepopulationandcommunity/personalandhouseholdfinances/expenditure/articles/whatactionsarepeopletakingbecauseoftherisingcostofliving/2022-08-05.

Chapter 2: The Audit

1. 'The 10 signs you might be settling in your relationship'. *Healing Honeys*. 2021. Available at: https://www.healing-honeys.com/blog/the-10-signs-you-might-be-settling-in-your-relationship.
2. 'How to discover your authentic self – at any age'. *TED Talks*. 2022. Available at: https://www.ted.com/talks/bevy_smith_how_to_discover_your_authentic_self_at_any_age/transcript.
3. 'Oracle Study Reveals Decision Making Paradox: More Data, Greater Uncertainty'. *BigDATAWire*. 2023. Available at: https://www.bigdatawire.com/2023/04/21/oracle-study-reveals-decision-making-paradox-more-data-greater-uncertainty/.
4. Anne-Laure Le Cunff, *Tiny Experiments: How to break free from a goal obsessed world*. Profile Books. 2025.

Chapter 3: Stick

1. 'Are You Suffering From 'Bore out?' *Happiful*. 2025. Available at: https://happiful.com/are-you-suffering-from-bore-out.
2. 'Warning to Managers: Survey Shows Most Workers Will Quit a Bad Boss'. *Business Wire*. 2022. Available at: https://www.businesswire.com/news/home/20220111005272/en/Warning-to-Managers-Survey-Shows-Most-Workers-Will-Quit-a-Bad-Boss.
3. 'Over two-thirds of UK workers have quit or considered quitting their office job due to poor management'. *HR News*. 2024. Available at: https://hrnews.co.uk/over-two-thirds-of-uk-workers-have-quit-or-considered-quitting-their-office-job-due-to-poor-management/.
4. 'Nearly half of UK employees don't see a clear path to progression'. *Iris*. 2022. Available at: https://www.iris.co.uk/news/nearly-half-of-uk-employees-dont-see-a-clear-path-to-progression/.
5. 'No path to progression felt by 50% of employees'. *HR Review*. 2022. Available at: https://hrreview.co.uk/hr-news/no-path-to-progression-felt-by-50-of-employees/144170.

ENDNOTES

6. Cindy Gallop, 'Hire Women: They do all the work and take none of the credit'. *PRWeek*. 2024. Available at: https://www.prweek.com/article/1871556/cindy-gallop-hire-women-work-none-credit.
7. Brianna Weist, *The Mountain Is You*. Thought Catalog Books. 2022.
8. Chip and Dan Heath, *The Power of Moments*. Simon & Schuster. 2017.
9. 'I tried the "romanticise your life" social trend as a busy mum of three – here's what happened (and how to try it for yourself)' *GoodToKnow*. 2024. Available at: https://www.goodto.com/family/i-tried-the-romanticising-my-life-social-trend-as-a-busy-mum-of-three-heres-what-happened-and-how-to-try-it-for-yourself.
10. 'The future will be shaped by optimists'. *TED Talks*. 2021. Available at: https://www.ted.com/talks/kevin_kelly_the_future_will_be_shaped_by_optimists.
11. Thasunda Brown Duckett, 'You rent your title, but you own your character'. LinkedIn. 2023. Available at: https://www.linkedin.com/pulse/you-rent-your-title-own-character-thasunda-brown-duckett/.
12. 'How to stop taking work so personally'. *Harvard Business Review*. 2023. Available at: https://hbr.org/2023/10/how-to-stop-taking-work-so-personally.
13. Dennis Reina and Michelle Reina, *Trust and Betrayal in the Workplace*. Berrett-Koehler. 1999.
14. 'Half of self-described people-pleasers think being this way makes life harder'. *YouGov US*. 2022. Available at: https://today.yougov.com/society/articles/50734-half-of-self-described-people-pleasers-think-being-this-way-makes-life-harder.
15. 'The Workforce State of Mind in 2025: How can employers address employee mental health today?' *Headspace*. 2025. Available at: https://organizations.headspace.com/blog/the-workforce-state-of-mind-in-2025-how-can-employers-address-employee-mental-health-today.
16. Gary Chapman and Paul White, *The 5 Languages of Appreciation in the Workplace*. Moody Publishers. 2011.
17. Chris Voss, *Never Split the Difference*. Random House Business. 2017.
18. 'Rising Strong with Brené Brown'. OWN. 2015. Available at: https://www.youtube.com/watch?v=M2SVHji3uYg&ab_channel=OWN.

Chapter 4: Twist

1. Daniel Pink, *The Power of Regret: How looking backward moves us forward*. Canongate Books. 2022.
2. 'The Confidence Gap'. *The Atlantic*. 2014. Available at: https://www.theatlantic.com/magazine/archive/2014/05/the-confidence-gap/359815/.

ENDNOTES

3. 'Impact of LinkedIn Recommendations on Hiring Decisions: 2025 Statistics and Data'. *Software Oasis*. 2024. Available at: https://softwareoasis.com/linkedin-recommendations-impact/.
4. 'Crowdfunding £20,000+ – the highs, lows & lessons', with Danielle from Flock Here *Starting the Conversation*. 2023. Available at: https://open.spotify.com/episode/4u7qbX69QFRLnwF1KcpoO9?si=ArMpEBlsQSWHQkgzvd49GQ.
5. 'How to find the person who can help you get ahead at work'. *TED Talks*. 2018. Available at: https://www.ted.com/talks/carla_harris_how_to_find_the_person_who_can_help_you_get_ahead_at_work?language=en.
6. Thomas Mussweiler, 'First impressions: never judge a book by its cover'. *think* at London Business School. 2021. Available at: https://www.london.edu/think/first-impressions-never-judge-a-book-by-its-cover.

Chapter 5: Tap Out

1. Aaron Flarin, 'Descend the corporate ladder'. Tiktok. 2024. Available at: https://vm.tiktok.com/ZNdfSeTkr/.
2. Joan C Williams, *Unbending Gender*. Oxford University Press. 1999.
3. 'The prevalence of workaholism: a systematic review and meta-analysis'. *Frontiers*. 2023. Available at: https://www.frontiersin.org/journals/psychology/articles/10.3389/fpsyg.2023.1252373/full.
4. '6 Signs You're Addicted to Stress'. *MelRobbins.com* 2023. Available at: https://open.spotify.com/episode/7xzCO4P4VBzG52y2EpxVrg?si=zZY39b6NTvqpvJbHBlZ4zg&nd=1&dlsi=ead1ac295df54545.
5. Dr Gabor Maté: 'The 5 Life Lessons People Learn Too Late, Why We Should Stop Trying To Live Longer & How Curiosity Leads To Compassion'. *DrChatterjee.com*. Available at: https://drchatterjee.com/dr-gabor-mate-the-5-life-lessons-people-learn-too-late-why-we-should-stop-trying-to-live-longer-how-curiosity-leads-to-compassion/.
6. 'The Problem With A Culture of Giving 110%'. *Health Care*. 2022. Available at: https://healthcare.utah.edu/integrative-health-wellness/resiliency-center/news/2022/08/problem-culture-of-giving-110.
7. Nate Daye, 'Giving 100% in the workplace?' Tiktok. 2024. Available at: https://vm.tiktok.com/ZNdfBtNfa/.
8. Scott Stillman, *I Don't Want To Grow Up*. Wild Soul Press. 2021.
9. Morgan Housel, *Same as Ever: Timeless lessons on risk, opportunity and living a good life*. Harriman House. 2023.

ENDNOTES

10. Mary Jelkovsky, '"For you" at the end of every sentence somebody tells me'. Tiktok. 2023. Available at: https://www.tiktok.com/@maryscupoftea/video/7387523970859420971?_t=ZN-8xe3JqLN6dq&_r=1.
11. 'Digital 2024: Global Overview Report'. *Datareportal*. 2024. Available at: https://datareportal.com/reports/digital-2024-global-overview-report.
12. 'The "Face-Down Phone Theory"'. *Unplugged*. 2024. Available at: https://unplugged.rest/blog/face-down-phone-theory.
13. 'The UK's workforce is one of the most dissatisfied in Europe'. *People Management* 2023. Available at: https://www.peoplemanagement.co.uk/article/1827408/uks-workforce-one-dissatisfied-europe.
14. National Center for Biotechnology Information, 'Psychological detachment from work during non-work time: linear or curvilinear relations with mental health and work engagement?' 2016. Available at: https://pmc.ncbi.nlm.nih.gov/articles/PMC4939862/.
15. 'Are you an integrator or a segmentor? Knowing the answer can help with work-life balance'. *Quartz*. 2022. Available at: https://qz.com/work/1349189/are-you-an-integrator-or-a-segmentor-knowing-the-answer-can-help-with-work-life-balance.
16. 'Tired of London, not life: what happens when you ditch the high-flying success – and stress – of the city grind'. *Stylist*. 2016. Available at: https://www.stylist.co.uk/life/careers/helen-russell-ditched-city-grind-less-stressful-more-fulfilling-london-denmark-lifestyle-stress-happiness-slow/45346.
17. 'The Big Idea: Why it's okay not to love your job'. *Guardian*. 2024. Available at: https://www.theguardian.com/books/2024/oct/14/the-big-idea-why-its-ok-not-to-love-your-job#:~:text=Love%20can%20distort%20your%20perception,looking%20for%20something%20better%20elsewhere.
18. 'Everything I Know About Love'. *BBC*. 2022. Available at: https://www.bbc.co.uk/iplayer/episodes/p0c70rlw/everything-i-know-about-love.

ACKNOWLEDGEMENTS

I couldn't finish this book without acknowledging some very special people who have helped behind the scenes to make this a reality. I'm so grateful of the support I received from everyone during this journey but I wanted to make a few specific acknowledgements:

To my wonderful editor Lola, it has been such a joy getting to have you by my side during this writing process. Your energy and enthusiasm has been infectious, and being able to bring this to life with your positive words of encouragement has made the journey so much more enjoyable. You've been as invested in making this book brilliant as I have, and for that I'll be forever grateful I got to work with you on this project. Thank you for you for keeping me on track, your continued dedication, and for always providing me with a fresh perspective I might not have seen alone.

To Kate, my agent and one of the first people who took a chance on me and my vision. You have been championing me since we first met, and I'm so pleased we've got to work together on not just one book, but two. A dream I never thought possible became real because of you. Thank you for being the incredible sounding board and thinking partner, and for always encouraging me to go bigger. From brainstorming ideas over drinks to

ACKNOWLEDGEMENTS

celebrating career milestones together, it's been so amazing to collaborate with you on this process.

To my incredible partner Tom, there is no one who has experienced this book journey as closely as you have, and I feel so fortunate to have had you on my front row supporting me every step of the way. Your support didn't look like notes on my first draft, your support was so much bigger. It was keeping me going whilst I navigated one of the hardest chapters of my life, all whilst reminding me that I could still create something brilliant at the same time. You have been the consistent loving foundation that enabled me to pour everything I had available into this book and I will never forget how much you have done for me. Thank you for always reminding me I can do anything, even when I didn't believe it myself.

To my beautiful friend Poonam, thank you for your constant reassurance and steady, guiding voice while I worked on one of my most life-changing projects of my life. You didn't just bring calm in stressful moments, you held space for me to reflect on the small and big steps I was taking that have shaped who I am today. Had you not offered suggestions and celebrated progress I might otherwise have missed, this book wouldn't carry the same level of honesty. Since the day I met you you've seen me clearly, believed in what I'm capable of, and have been a safe space for me to express myself. Not everyone is lucky enough to receive this, so I will always treasure having you in my life and on this journey.

To my therapist Jaspreet, we began working together during the height of my writing, at a time when I was navigating an incredibly difficult personal season. You helped me move through identity shifts, sadness, and grief, while continually reminding me that my value is not defined by professional achievements. Thank you for making me feel emotionally, mentally, and

ACKNOWLEDGEMENTS

physically safe, and for always communicating with such care. Our work together has been central to building a healthier relationship with work and reminding me that so much of what I thought I needed was already within me. Connecting my body and mind through your somatic practices has allowed me to show up more authentically, both in writing and in daily life. I'm deeply grateful for the time we shared each week, guiding me toward a more aligned version of myself.

To Gemma, my sister, one of the most inspiring people I know. You didn't just pave the way through our childhood years, you have showcased what it looks like to be ambitious and brave, courageous and caring, and to never follow a path that wasn't right for you. You've followed your curiosities even when it meant challenging the status quo, stood up for people who couldn't stand up for themselves, and made sacrifices in service of a bigger purpose. Every time I sat down to write this book, I thought of you and all you have pushed through to be where you are. I know you will continue to follow what's important to you and inspire many more people. Thanks for always being unapologetically you.